"Filled with thought-provoking phrases and quotes, this book will motivate and inspire us to develop a deeper, closer relationship with our Lord and Savior. *Lists to Live By: The Christian Collection* is a provocative read that will definitely stimulate your thoughts and beliefs."

DR. GARY SMALLEY
AUTHOR OF *THE DNA OF RELATIONSHIPS*

"The Lists to Live By books are famous for putting wise thoughts into easy to remember lists. Now the compilers have come up with an even more valuable book—a Christian collection. These lists will help you live each day for God's pleasure. Read them, apply them, and you will discover what Christian living is all about."

DR. KENNETH N. TAYLOR
TRANSLATOR OF *THE LIVING BIBLE*

"This book offers concise, perspective-giving and soul-feeding insights. In a format that makes for quick reading, it takes us to God's Word, which has a power to change us that no other words have."

RANDY ALCORN
BESTSELLING AUTHOR OF *DEADLINE*

"What we really need to make it through life is a little courage and a lot of wisdom. This helpful book will keep your wisdom tank full for all occasions."

DR. JOSEPH M. STOWELL
PRESIDENT OF MOODY BIBLE INSTITUTE

"When time is a premium and the Bible is to be our daily food, it's great to have a book like this that gives practical nuggets and rich insights."

KAY ARTHUR
AUTHOR AND CO-CEO OF PRECEPT MINISTRIES INTERNATIONAL

LISTS *to* LIVE *By*

THE CHRISTIAN COLLECTION

FOR EVERYTHING THAT REALLY MATTERS

COMPILED BY

ALICE GRAY

STEVE STEPHENS

JOHN VAN DIEST

Multnomah® Publishers *Sisters, Oregon*

LISTS TO LIVE BY: THE CHRISTIAN COLLECTION
published by Multnomah Publishers, Inc.

© 2004 by Alice Gray, Steve Stephens, and John Van Diest
International Standard Book Number: 1-59052-370-9 (paperback)
1-59052-499-3 (hardback)

Cover design by The DesignWorks Group

Unless otherwise indicated, Scripture quotations are from:
The Holy Bible, New International Version
© 1973, 1984 by International Bible Society,
used by permission of Zondervan Publishing House
Other Scripture quotations are from:
New American Standard Bible (NASB)
© 1960, 1977 by the Lockman Foundation
The Holy Bible, King James Version (KJV)
Holy Bible, New Living Translation (NLT)
© 1996. Used by permission of Tyndale House Publishers, Inc.
All rights reserved.
Revised Standard Version Bible (RSV)
© 1946, 1952 by the Division of Christian Education
of the National Council of the Churches of Christ
in the United States of America
New Revised Standard Version Bible (NRSV)
© 1989 by the Division of Christian Education
of the National Council of the Churches of Christ
in the United States of America

Multnomah is a trademark of Multnomah Publishers, Inc.,
and is registered in the U.S. Patent and Trademark Office.
The colophon is a trademark of Multnomah Publishers, Inc.

For information:
MULTNOMAH PUBLISHERS, INC.
POST OFFICE BOX 1720
SISTERS, OREGON 97759

Library of Congress Cataloging-in-Publication Data

Lists to live by : the Christian collection for everthing that really matters / compiled by Alice Gray,
Steve Stephens, John Van Diest.
    p. cm.
  ISBN 1-59052-370-9 (pbk.)
  ISBN 1-59052-499-3
  1. Christian life. I. Gray, Alice, 1939- II. Stephens, Steve. III. Van Diest, John.
  BV4501.3.L57 2004
  248.4--dc22

                    2004015657

05 06 07 08 09 10—10 9 8 7 6 5 4

CONTENTS

INTRODUCTION
LISTS MAKE A POWERFUL DIFFERENCE!

ESPECIALLY WHEN THEY ARE...

Life-changing
Influential
Stimulating
Trustworthy
Significant

The selections for this newest collection in the bestselling Lists to Live By series were specially chosen to refresh, challenge, and encourage you. As you read through them, we hope the thoughts of so many varied authors will deepen your faith and nurture your soul. By grouping certain lists together, we've made it easier for you to discover a new appreciation for timeless topics such as worship, prayer, marriage, family, virtue, success, wisdom, comfort, and eternal hope.

We've tried to catch the beauty of simplicity by taking powerful ideas and expressing them in only a few words. If it is true that the best gifts come in small packages, then reading this book will be like unwrapping more than two hundred small gifts that are filled with extraordinary inspiration.

Even though you may be rushed with many demands and responsibilities, please don't hurry through this book. Find a cozy corner, settle back in a comfortable chair, and turn the pages leisurely. Linger over your favorite lists; meditate on the profound wisdom; embrace the joy. They will energize your daily walk and ultimately enrich your life.

ALICE GRAY   STEVE STEPHENS   JOHN VAN DIEST

1
Faith

Trusting the One who is worthy

THE GREATEST REASONS FOR FAITH

God	*the greatest lover*
so loved	*the greatest degree*
the world	*the greatest company*
that he gave	*the greatest act*
his only begotten Son	*the greatest gift*
that whosoever	*the greatest opportunity*
believes	*the greatest simplicity*
in him	*the greatest attraction*
should not perish	*the greatest promise*
but	*the greatest difference*
have	*the greatest certainty*
everlasting life	*the greatest possession*

AUTHOR UNKNOWN
BASED ON JOHN 3:16

THE ULTIMATE GOOD IN
THE "GOOD NEWS"

SALVATION
is not good news if it only saves from hell
and not for God.

FORGIVENESS
is not good news if it only gives relief from guilt
and doesn't open the way to God.

JUSTIFICATION
is not good news if it only makes us acceptable to God
but doesn't bring fellowship with God.

REDEMPTION
is not good news if it only liberates us from bondage
but doesn't bring us to God.

ADOPTION
is not good news if it only puts us in the Father's family
but not in His arms.

THE ULTIMATE GOOD NEWS IS GOD HIMSELF.

JOHN PIPER
ADAPTED FROM "THE PASSION OF JESUS CHRIST"

IF JESUS IS YOUR SAVIOR

If Jesus is your Savior…

Your sins are forgiven.

Your guilt is atoned for.

Your past is removed.

Your future is secured.

You have peace in your heart.

You have purpose to your step.

You have a song on your lips.

You are saved from hell.

You are right with God.

You are going to heaven.

ANNE GRAHAM LOTZ
FROM "JUST GIVE ME JESUS"

A VIOLENT GRACE

HE WAS BORN TO DIE
so I could be born to new life.

HE SUFFERED TEMPTATION
so I can experience victory.

HE WAS BETRAYED
so I might know His faithfulness.

HE WAS ARRESTED AND BOUND
so I could be rescued from bondage.

HE STOOD TRIAL ALONE
so I might have an advocate.

HE WAS WOUNDED
so I could be healed.

HE ENDURED MOCKERY
so I could know dignity and joy.

HE WAS CONDEMNED
so the truth could set me free.

HE WAS CROWNED WITH THORNS
so I might crown Him with praise.

HE WAS NAILED TO THE CROSS
so I might escape judgment.

HE WAS STRETCHED OUT BETWEEN THIEVES
so I could know the reach of love.

HE SUFFERED THIRST
so I can drink living water.

HE SAID, "IT IS FINISHED,"
so I could begin my walk of faith.

HE WAS GOD'S LAMB, SLAIN,
so I could claim His sacrifice as my own.

HE WAS FORSAKEN BY THE FATHER
so I would never be rejected.

HE CHOSE THE SHAME OF WEAKNESS
so I can know the hope of glory.

HE SHED HIS BLOOD
so I can be white as snow.

HIS HEART WAS PIERCED
so mine could be made whole.

HE DIED AND WAS BURIED
so the grave could not hold me.

HE ROSE AGAIN
so I might experience eternal life.

HE IS KNOWN BY HIS SCARS
so I will take up my cross and follow Him.

MICHAEL CARD
FROM "A VIOLENT GRACE"

GRACE MEANS...

YOU ARE BEYOND CONDEMNATION.

So now there is no condemnation for those who belong to Christ Jesus.

ROMANS 8:1

YOU ARE DELIVERED FROM THE LAW.

But now we have been released from the law,
for we died with Christ, and we are no longer captive to its power.

ROMANS 7:6

YOU ARE NEAR GOD.

But now you belong to Christ Jesus.
Though you once were far away from God,
now you have been brought near to him because of the blood of Christ.

EPHESIANS 2:13

YOU ARE DELIVERED FROM THE POWER OF EVIL.

For he has rescued us from the one who rules in the kingdom of darkness...

COLOSSIANS 1:13

YOU ARE A MEMBER OF HIS KINGDOM.

...and he has brought us into the Kingdom of his dear Son.

COLOSSIANS 1:13

YOU ARE JUSTIFIED.

Therefore since we have been made right in God's sight by faith, we have
peace with God because of what Jesus Christ our Lord has done for us.

ROMANS 5:1

YOU ARE PERFECT.

For by that one offering he perfected forever all those whom he is making holy.

HEBREWS 10:14

YOU HAVE BEEN ADOPTED.

So you should not be like cowering, fearful slaves. You should behave instead like
God's very own children, adopted into his family—calling him "Father, dear Father."

ROMANS 8:15

YOU HAVE ACCESS TO GOD AT ANY MOMENT.

Now all of us…may come to the Father through the same Holy Spirit
because of what Christ has done for us.

EPHESIANS 2:18

YOU ARE A PART OF HIS PRIESTHOOD.

You are God's holy priests, who offer spiritual sacrifices that
please him because of Jesus Christ.

I PETER 2:5

YOU WILL NEVER BE ABANDONED.

God has said, "I will never fail you. I will never forsake you."

HEBREWS 13:5

YOU HAVE AN IMPERISHABLE INHERITANCE.

For God has reserved a priceless inheritance for his children. It is kept
in heaven for you, pure and undefiled, beyond the reach of change and decay.

I PETER 1:4

YOU ARE A PARTNER WITH CHRIST IN LIFE.

And when Christ, who is your real life, is revealed to the whole world,
you will share in all his glory.

COLOSSIANS 3:4

MAX LUCADO
FROM "IN THE GRIP OF GRACE"
SCRIPTURES ARE FROM THE NEW LIVING TRANSLATION

FAITH

INTIMACY WITH GOD

IT'S ABOUT...

† A deep and abiding sense of His nearness on the journey.

† An unshakable confidence that only His abiding presence can give.

† Courage in the face of previously intimidating encounters.

† Closeness that enables your spirit to commune with Him, anywhere, anytime, regardless.

† Meeting Him in places you may have never dreamed of...in the most heated of seductions, in the midst of suffering, and in acts of unflinching surrender.

JOSEPH M. STOWELL
FROM "SIMPLY JESUS"

HOW TO LISTEN TO GOD

Expectantly

Quietly

Patiently

Actively

Confidently

Dependently

Openly

Attentively

Carefully

Submissively

Gratefully

Reverently

CHARLES STANLEY
FROM "HOW TO LISTEN TO GOD"

OUR RESPONSE TO GOD

HEAR HIM AFRESH.

God never hides the truth. He is always open and honest with us. We are the ones who tend to overlook, or not hear, all that God is saying. He is always taking the initiative to make His assignment known, and we must be actively alert to receive it.

BELIEVE HIM WHOLEHEARTEDLY.

We must determine that God is everything He says He is and will do everything He says He will do for us—if we let Him. As He calls us to accomplish the impossible, we know He'll provide everything we need.

ADJUST TO HIM—UNCONDITIONALLY—

in our lives and in our churches, in order to join in God's revealed activity. God has the right to require and to make these adjustments in us in order to conform us to Himself and to His will—regardless of how long the process takes.

OBEY HIM—

immediately and in faith, as He leads us. He will then accomplish His purposes through us as we reach out not only to our immediate community, but to the world beyond.

HENRY BLACKABY
ADAPTED FROM "WHAT THE SPIRIT IS SAYING TO THE CHURCHES"

GOD IS WORTHY OF OUR FAITH

* He is your protector…
    when you feel lost, weary, and afraid
* He is good…
    when it's time to renew your perspective
* He is holy…
    when you yearn for someone greater than yourself
* He is your guide…
    when you need guidance
* He is near…
    when you long to feel His presence
* He is a faithful friend…
    when you yearn for His company
* He is just…
    when you need to leave justice in God's hands
* He is all-powerful…
    when the battle is too much for you
* He is grace…
    when you need forgiveness
* He is love…
    when you feel orphaned by life
* He is merciful…
    when you need a Savior
* He is majestic…
    when you're filled with awe by His creativity

LISA TAWN BERGREN
CONDENSED FROM "GOD ENCOUNTERS"

WHAT FAITH LOOKS LIKE

Take the first step in faith.
You don't have to see the whole staircase,
just take the first step.
MARTIN LUTHER KING JR.

༄

The strengthening of faith comes through
staying with it in the hour of trial.
CATHERINE MARSHALL

༄

For the believer, there is no question;
for the nonbeliever, there is no answer.
ANONYMOUS

༄

The light of God surrounds me,
The love of God enfolds me,
The power of God protects me,
The presence of God watches over me.
PRAYER CARD

Faith never knows where it is being led,
but it loves and knows the One who is leading.
OSWALD CHAMBERS

❧

I believe in Christianity as I believe that the sun has risen.
Not only because I see it, but because I see everything by it.
C. S. LEWIS

❧

Although the threads of my life
have often seemed knotted,
I know, by faith,
that on the other side of the embroidery
there is a crown.
CORRIE TEN BOOM

❧

Trust the past to God's mercy
The present to God's love
The future to God's providence.
ST. AUGUSTINE

QUESTIONS FOR THOSE WHO DOUBT

HOW COULD THERE BE CREATION WITHOUT A CREATOR?
Spontaneous generation has never been proved.

HOW COULD THERE BE LIFE THAT NEVER CAME FROM LIFE?
Science says that life can only come from life.

HOW COULD THERE BE DESIGN WITHOUT A DESIGNER?
There is too much to assume everything is an accident.

HOW COULD THERE BE LAW (LAW OF GRAVITY,
LAW OF PRODUCTION, ETC.) WITHOUT A LAWGIVER?
We have many laws. If God didn't give them, who did?

LEROY BROWNLOW
FROM "A PSALM IN MY HEART"

I SEE GOD IN...

~ The majesty of His creation

~ The life of Jesus Christ

~ Answered prayer

~ A humble spirit

~ The miracle of a newborn baby

~ The innocence of young children

~ A mother's tears for her child

~ A father's embrace of his child

~ The gift of love

~ Giving forgiveness

~ The joy of reconciliation

~ Rejoicing with one another

~ Seeking God's pure thoughts

~ Serving one another

~ Sharing kindnesses

~ Giving to those in need

~ Binding wounds of the unloved

~ God's daily guidance

~ Sacrificial deeds

~ Hearing, "Thank you"

PAUL ELLISON
PASTOR AND BIBLE TEACHER

FAITH IS...

Recognizing that God is the Lord of time
when my idea of timing doesn't agree with His.

Remembering I am God's priceless treasure
when I feel utterly worthless.

Ceasing to worry—leaving the future to the God
who controls the future.

Accepting the truth that in spite of the wreckage
I've caused and grieve over, God,
who has wiped the slate clean, delights in me.

Depending on God's enablement to live
and be blessed in a fallen world
rather than insisting He change it.

Trusting that God is doing His work in me
when I feel inwardly cold, hollow, lifeless, deserted
and I long for reassuring feelings.

PAMELA REEVE
SELECTED FROM "FAITH IS..."

WHAT WE NEED

WE DON'T NEED "ANSWERS";
we need Jesus.

✝

WE DON'T NEED DETAILS;
we need a Guide.

✝

WE DON'T NEED AN ITINERARY;
we need His steady hand on our shoulder,
leading us through the perilous terrain
of a fallen world under enemy control.

LARRY LIBBY AND STEVE HALLIDAY
FROM "NO MATTER WHAT, NO MATTER WHERE"

50 FAITH-BUILDING BOOKS
ARRANGED IN RANDOM ORDER

1. *What's So Amazing About Grace?* by Philip Yancey
2. *A Shepherd Looks at Psalm 23* by Phillip Keller
3. *No Wonder They Call Him the Savior* by Max Lucado
4. *The Purpose-Driven Life* by Rick Warren
5. *Mere Christianity* by C. S. Lewis
6. *The Pursuit of Holiness* by Jerry Bridges
7. *Faith Is…* by Pamela Reeve
8. *The Case for Christ* by Lee Strobel
9. *My Utmost for His Highest* by Oswald Chambers
10. *Fresh Wind, Fresh Fire* by Jim Cymbala and Dean Merrill
11. *More Than a Carpenter* by Josh McDowell
12. *The Chronicles of Narnia* series by C. S. Lewis
13. *Experiencing God* by Henry T. Blackaby and Claude V. King
14. *The Practice of the Presence of God* by Brother Lawrence
15. *Peace with God* by Billy Graham
16. *Improving Your Serve* by Charles R. Swindoll
17. *The Sacred Romance* by Brent Curtis and John Eldredge
18. *Secrets of the Vine* by Bruce Wilkinson
19. *The Ragamuffin Gospel* by Brennan Manning
20. *In His Steps* by Charles M. Sheldon
21. *The Grace and Truth Paradox* by Randy Alcorn
22. *With Christ in the School of Prayer* by Andrew Murray
23. *Heaven* by Joni Eareckson Tada
24. *The Cost of Discipleship* by Dietrich Bonhoeffer
25. *The Power of a Praying Wife* by Stormie Omartian
26. *Hinds' Feet on High Places* by Hannah Hurnard
27. *Know What You Believe* by Paul E. Little

28. *My Heart—Christ's Home* by Robert Boyd Munger

29. *This Present Darkness* by Frank E. Peretti

30. *How Now Shall We Live?* by Charles W. Colson

31. *The Pilgrim's Progress* by John Bunyan

32. *The Wounded Healer* by Henri J. M. Nouwen

33. *The Pursuit of God* by A. W. Tozer

34. *The Left Behind* series by Tim LaHaye and Jerry B. Jenkins

35. *Desiring God* by John Piper

36. *Knowing God* by J. I. Packer

37. *Out of the Saltshaker & Into the World* by Rebecca Manley Pippert

38. *The Imitation of Christ* by Thomas à Kempis

39. *The Christian's Secret of a Happy Life* by Hannah Whitall Smith

40. *True Spirituality* by Francis A. Schaeffer

41. *The Divine Conspiracy* by Dallas Willard

42. *Celebration of Discipline* by Richard J. Foster

43. *The Screwtape Letters* by C. S. Lewis

44. *The Brothers Karamazov* by Fyodor Dostoyevsky

45. *Streams in the Desert* by Mrs. Charles E. Cowman

46. *A Severe Mercy* by Sheldon Vanauken

47. *The Lord of the Rings* trilogy by J. R. R. Tolkien

48. *Redeeming Love* by Francine Rivers

49. *Through Gates of Splendor* by Elisabeth Elliot

50. *The Holiness of God* by R. C. Sproul

COMPILED BY THE EDITORS

2
Growing Deeper and Stronger

Experiencing a richer daily walk

GOD WILL REWARD YOU

For seeking Him through spiritual acts such as prayer and fasting.
MATTHEW 6:6

For submitting to your employer as a faithful servant.
MATTHEW 24:45-47

For self-denial in His service.
MATTHEW 16:24-27

For serving those in need in His name.
MARK 9:41

For suffering for His name and reputation.
LUKE 6:22-23

For sacrifices you make for Him.
LUKE 6:35

For sharing your time, talent, and treasure to further His kingdom.
MATTHEW 6:3-4

BRUCE WILKINSON
CONDENSED FROM "A LIFE GOD REWARDS"

DEVELOPING SELF-DISCIPLINE

1) START WITH SMALL THINGS.
Learning self-discipline in the little things of life prepares
us for big successes. On the other hand, those who are
undisciplined in small matters will likely be undisciplined
in more important matters.

2) GET YOURSELF ORGANIZED.
Make a schedule, however detailed or general you are
comfortable with, and stick to it. Have a to-do list of tasks
you need to accomplish.

3) DON'T CONSTANTLY SEEK TO BE ENTERTAINED.
When you have free time, do things that are productive
instead of merely entertaining. Read a good book, listen to
classical music, take a walk, or have a conversation with
someone.

4) BE ON TIME.
Being punctual marks a life that is organized. It reveals a
person whose desires, activities, and responsibilities are
under control, allowing him to get where he needs to be
when he needs to be there.

5) KEEP YOUR WORD.
If you say you're going to do something, do it—when you
said you would do it and how you said you would do it.
When you make commitments, see them through. That
calls for the discipline to properly evaluate whether you
have the time and capability to do something.

6) DO THE MOST DIFFICULT TASKS FIRST.

Most people do just the opposite, spending their time doing the easier, low-priority tasks. But when they run out of time (and energy), the difficult, high-priority tasks are left undone.

7) FINISH WHAT YOU START.

If you start something, finish it. Therein lies an important key to developing self-discipline.

8) ACCEPT CORRECTION.

Correction helps you develop self-discipline by showing you what you need to avoid. Thus, it should not be rejected but accepted gladly.

9) PRACTICE SELF-DENIAL.

Learn to say no to your feelings and impulses. Occasionally deny yourself pleasures that are perfectly legitimate for you to enjoy.

10) WELCOME RESPONSIBILITY.

Volunteer to do things that need to be done. That will force you to have your life organized enough to have time for such projects.

JOHN F. MACARTHUR
CONDENSED FROM "THE PILLARS OF CHRISTIAN CHARACTER"

GOD IS SEEKING YOU

✣ HE'S SEEKING YOU
so you can know just how amazing He is.

✣ HE'S SEEKING YOU
so you can know what you're created to do.

✣ HE'S SEEKING YOU
so you can find Him and value Him with all your heart.

✣ HE'S SEEKING YOU
because He's God…and He knows you can't live without Him.

LOUIE GIGLIO
FROM "THE AIR I BREATHE"

YIELDING TO GOD

⚜ Yielding means continuing to grow close to God.

⚜ Yielding means doing everything in Jesus' name.

⚜ Yielding means listening to the voice of our Lord as He guides us.

⚜ Yielding means undergoing a refinement process, which strips away the flaws and distractions that hinder intimacy with Him.

⚜ Yielding means abandoning ourselves to God in contented trust.

SHIRLEY DOBSON
ADAPTED FROM "CERTAIN PEACE IN UNCERTAIN TIMES"

SPIRITUAL DISCIPLINES

1. PRAYER
Pray without ceasing.

2. MEDITATION
Meditate on God's Word day and night.

3. SILENCE
Be still and know that God is near.

4. SIMPLICITY
Celebrate the simple things.

5. DEVOTIONS AND BIBLE READING
Study and let your heart grow.

6. CHURCH ATTENDANCE
Gather together regularly with believers.

7. ACTS OF WORSHIP
Worship the Lord in all you do.

8. GIVING AND SERVING
Take on the heart of a servant.

9. CONFESSION
Confess your sins to one another.

10. THANKSGIVING
Give thanks for all things.

11. CONTENTMENT
Learn to be content in whatever your circumstances.

12. FORGIVENESS
Forgive as God has forgiven you.

13. HARMONY
Live in harmony with all people.

14. LOVE AND COMPASSION AND KINDNESS
Choose to walk in love.

15. ENCOURAGEMENT
Encourage and build up others every chance you get.

DR. STEVE STEPHENS
AUTHOR AND SEMINAR SPEAKER

SIX STEPS TO SPIRITUAL REVIVAL

1. *Humble yourself.* Let the brightness and beauty of His holy presence reveal how dependent you are upon His forgiveness and grace.

2. *Pray with every fiber of your being.* Call on the Lord with a desperate intensity, refusing to be distracted by the cares and toys of our shallow culture.

3. *Seek God's face above all else.* If you sense His nearness, don't let Him pass on by. Cry out for His presence as if crying out for water in arid wilderness.

4. *Turn from all known sin.* Allow God's Spirit the time and opportunity to search the very depths of your heart.

5. *Pray with fellow believers regularly, with your hearts "in one accord" regarding the issues of faith that matter most.* Discover the energy, joy, and power of joining your prayer to that of two or three others—or maybe thousands!

6. *Persevere in all these things.* Hold onto faith, patience, and steadfast hope in the face of all that Satan or a godless world might throw at you.

PAT ROBERTSON
FROM "SIX STEPS TO SPIRITUAL REVIVAL"

GOD'S PLAN FOR GROWTH

† Devote yourself to truth.

† Commit your heart to worship.

† Partake regularly of communion.

† Practice consistent prayer.

† Get excited about what God can do.

† Share all you have with each other.

† Give to anyone in need.

† Meet together daily.

† Develop hospitality and invite others to your home.

† Embrace a joyful and positive attitude.

† Praise God in all things.

DR. LUKE
ACTS 2:42–47

THE VALUE OF REMEMBERING

Remembering…

GIVES REASSURANCE WHEN WE ARE DISCOURAGED—

*I remember the days of old, I meditate on all that thou hast done;
I muse on what thy hands have wrought.*

PSALM 143:5

REMINDS US THAT GOD IS GOD—

*Remember the former things of old; for I am God, and there is no other;
I am God, and there is none like me.*

ISAIAH 46:9

STRENGTHENS US FOR HARD TIMES—

*But recall the former days when, after you were enlightened,
you endured a hard struggle with sufferings.*

HEBREWS 10:32

ENABLES US TO BUILD ON GOOD, OLD FOUNDATIONS—

*Your ancient ruins shall be rebuilt; you shall raise up the
foundations of many generations; you shall be called the
repairer of the breach, the restorer of streets to dwell in.*

ISAIAH 58:12

LETS US RECOVER LONG-LOST, PRECIOUS TRUTHS—

*Thus says the Lord: "Stand by the roads, and look, and ask for the ancient
paths, where the good way is; and walk in it, and find rest for your souls."*

JEREMIAH 6:16

HELPS US STAY HUMBLE UNDER GOD'S MIGHTY HAND—

*You shall remember that you were a servant in the land of Egypt,
and the Lord your God brought you out thence with a mighty
hand and an outstretched arm.*

DEUTERONOMY 5:15

TEACHES US THE LESSONS OF GOD'S GREAT DEEDS—

Do you not yet perceive? Do you not remember the five loaves
of the five thousand, and how many baskets you gathered?

MATTHEW 16:9

WARNS US AGAINST THE FOLLY OF THE FOOLISH—

Remember Lot's wife.

LUKE 17:32

STIMULATES REPENTANCE—

Remember then what you received and heard;
keep that, and repent.

REVELATION 3:3

SHOWS WHAT IS TRULY UNIQUE AND MARVELOUS—

Ask now of the days that are past, which were before you,
since the day that God created man upon the earth,
and ask from one end of heaven to the other,
whether such a great thing as this has ever happened or was ever heard of.

DEUTERONOMY 4:32

POINTS TO A GLORIOUS NEW AND UNPRECEDENTED FUTURE—

Remember not the former things, nor consider the things of old.
Behold, I am doing a new thing.

ISAIAH 43:18–19

JOHN PIPER
FROM "A GODWARD LIFE"
SCRIPTURES ARE FROM THE REVISED STANDARD VERSION

10 STRATEGIES TO
STRENGTHEN YOUR BELIEFS

State with confidence and boldness: *God has endowed me with everything I need to be what He wants me to be and to accomplish what He wants me to accomplish.*

Remind yourself often of the Lord's promise to make a way when there seems to be no way.

Highlight every verse in your Bible that deals with courage, confidence, faith, and believing.

Pray the promises of God.

Visualize and affirm your assets.

Make a list of character qualities you want to develop, and then memorize your list.

Actively replace negative thoughts and statements with positive thoughts and statements.

When an obstacle arises, state boldly: *If God is for me, who can be against me?*

When you are feeling harassed by Satan, say aloud: *Father God, I want to thank You that You are greater in me than anything Satan can do to me.*

Remind yourself continually: *God is with me in this.*

CHARLES STANLEY
FROM "SUCCESS GOD'S WAY"

DESIRE FOR SPIRITUAL GROWTH

* May I never press you for temporal blessings;

* May I never think I prosper unless my soul prospers;

* May I seek first thy kingdom and its righteousness;

* May I value things in relation to eternity;

* May my spiritual welfare be my chief solicitude;

* May I seek my happiness in Thy favor, image,
  presence, service.

ARTHUR BENNETT
ADAPTED FROM "THE VALLEY OF VISION"

GUIDELINES FOR GIVING

→ GIVE TRUSTINGLY—focus on God's faithfulness instead of on what you don't have.

→ GIVE EXPECTANTLY—know that God will provide for all your needs according to His riches in glory.

→ GIVE JOYFULLY—realize that God blesses giving and trust.

→ GIVE GRATEFULLY—acknowledge all the blessings that God has given to you.

→ GIVE LAVISHLY—know that you cannot outgive God!

SUSAN HUEY WALES
FROM "STANDING ON THE PROMISES"

RESOLUTIONS

❖ I RESOLVE to examine carefully and constantly what is that one thing in me that causes me in the least to doubt the love of God; and to direct all my forces against it.

❖ I RESOLVE not only to refrain from an air of dislike, fretfulness, and anger in conversation, but to exhibit an air of love, cheerfulness, and gentleness.

❖ I RESOLVE to study the Scriptures so steadily, constantly, and frequently that I may plainly perceive myself to grow in the knowledge of them.

❖ I RESOLVE never to do any manner of thing, whether in soul or body, except what tends to the glory of God.

❖ I RESOLVE frequently to take some deliberate action, which seems most unlikely to be done, for the glory of God.

❖ I RESOLVE never to give over, nor in the least to slacken, my fight with my corruptions, however unsuccessful I may be.

❖ I RESOLVE never to act as if I were any way my own, but entirely and altogether God's.

❖ I RESOLVE to ask every night as I am going to bed in what way I have been negligent, what sin I have committed, and in what way I have denied myself; also to do this at the end of every week, month, and year.

❖ I RESOLVE to live with all my might, while I do live.

JONATHAN EDWARDS
THEOLOGIAN AND PHILOSOPHER

10 PRINCIPLES OF DISCIPLINE

1) To learn you must love discipline.

2) Discipline begins with small things done daily.

3) Discipline is the secret behind most success.

4) The first step to discipline is making up your mind.

5) Discipline involves using your time productively.

6) If you want to achieve excellence, begin with discipline.

7) Motivation can fade. Discipline prevails.

8) Discipline is not good at making excuses.

9) Discipline acquires good habits, while it abandons bad habits.

10) Discipline is the art of balance, consistency, and perseverance.

BRUCE AND STAN
ADAPTED FROM "GOD IS IN THE SMALL STUFF"

A DEVOTED HEART IS...

AN UNDERSTANDING HEART—
Incline your heart to understanding.
PROVERBS 2:2, NASB

A TRUSTING HEART—
Trust in the LORD with all your heart.
PROVERBS 3:5

A GUARDED HEART—
Above all else, guard your heart.
PROVERBS 4:23, NLT

A TRANQUIL HEART—
A tranquil heart is life to the body.
PROVERBS 14:30, NASB

A HAPPY HEART—
For the happy heart, life is a continual feast.
PROVERBS 15:15, NLT

A RIGHTEOUS HEART—
The heart of the righteous ponders how to answer.
PROVERBS 15:28, NASB

A WISE HEART—
A wise man's heart guides his mouth.
PROVERBS 16:23

A DISCERNING HEART—
The heart of the discerning acquires knowledge.
PROVERBS 18:15

KING SOLOMON
FROM THE HOLY BIBLE

A CHARGE TO KEEP

- ❦ GLORIFY GOD.

- ❦ SAVE SOULS.

- ❦ SERVE OTHERS.

- ❦ FULFILL MY CALLING.

- ❦ USE MY GIFTS AND TALENTS.

- ❦ DO MY MASTER'S WILL.

ADAPTED FROM CHARLES WESLEY
PASTOR AND HYMN WRITER

3

God and His Word

Finding the source of joy and peace

WHO THE BIBLE SAYS YOU ARE

❧ You are an heir of God and a coheir with Christ.

ROMANS 8:17

❧ You are eternal, like an angel.

1 CORINTHIANS 9:25

❧ You have a crown that will last forever.

1 CORINTHIANS 9:25

❧ You are a holy priest.

1 PETER 2:5

❧ You are a treasured possession.

EXODUS 19:5

❧ You were chosen before the creation of the world.

EPHESIANS 1:4

❧ You were destined for praise, fame, and honor.

DEUTERONOMY 26:19

❧ You are God's child.

1 JOHN 3:1

MAX LUCADO
FROM "HE STILL MOVES STONES"

WHAT THE BIBLE DOES

- PROVIDES DIRECTION

- TEACHES TRUTH

- BUILDS FAITH

- CHANGES LIVES

- IMPROVES CHARACTER

- CALMS FEARS

- COMFORTS HURTS

- INSTILLS HOPE

- PREPARES ONE FOR ETERNITY

LOREN FISCHER
PASTOR AND SEMINARY PROFESSOR

PUT THE BIBLE IN YOUR HEART

* **STUDY IT WITH HEART.**

  Approach Scripture with enthusiasm! The psalmist describes the anticipation of learning God's precepts this way: "How sweet are Your words to my taste! Yes, sweeter than honey to my mouth!" (Psalm 119:103, NASB)

* **TAKE IT TO HEART.**

  I have lived long enough to realize that I desperately need truth in my life. By now, I've gotten just enough intelligence to be dangerous. I've gotten just enough of man's wisdom to know it isn't trustworthy. I need His yes and no, His light to expose my darkness, His precepts to steel my convictions. His Word provides all that.

* **LEARN IT BY HEART.**

  Tradition tells us that the Jewish mothers of the first century taught their children to pray, "Into Your hands I commit my spirit" (Psalm 31:5). During Jesus' last hour on the cross, He repeated that same Scripture, most likely having memorized it as a child at Mary's knee. I don't know of any discipline that will transform thoughts better than memorizing the Word. How urgently we need truth riveted to our hearts.

CHARLES R. SWINDOLL
FROM "INSIGHTS" NEWSLETTER

SEVEN STEPS FOR
MEMORIZING SCRIPTURE

1. DECIDE IT IS A PRIORITY FOR YOUR LIFE.
   We will not sacrifice to achieve that which is unimportant.

2. SET A REALISTIC GOAL.
   Attempting to learn too much too quickly will result in frustration. Memorizing too little will bring boredom.

3. CHOOSE VERSES THAT TOUCH YOUR HEART.
   When God communicates to you through a passage, it is much easier to remember those verses.

4. CREATE A LEARNING ENVIRONMENT AROUND YOU.
   Write out passages on note cards, and tape them to your mirror, treadmill, desk, or dashboard.

5. INCORPORATE THE VERSES INTO YOUR DAILY LIFE.
   Reflect on memorized verses when pressed to make a decision, when responding to an unkind

person, when encouraging your family, or when you are under stress. Remember—if you don't use it, you'll lose it.

6. IF POSSIBLE, LEARN SCRIPTURE WITH OTHERS.
You can encourage one another, provide account-ability, and even make reviewing passages into a game or contest. This especially works in the context of families.

7. REVIEW, REVIEW, REVIEW.
It is work to learn God's Word, and the enemy will oppose and offer distraction. Scripture memory is a discipline that will change your life, but it is a discipline.

THOUGHTS ABOUT GOD'S WORD

The Bible is a window in this prison-world,
through which we may look into eternity.
TIMOTHY DWIGHT

❧

Nobody ever outgrows Scripture;
the book widens and deepens with our years.
CHARLES HADDON SPURGEON

❧

As in paradise, God walks in the Holy Scriptures, seeking man.
SAINT AMBROSE

❧

Be astounded that God should have written to us.
ANTONY OF EGYPT

❧

The gospel is not only the most important message in all of history;
it is the only essential message in all of history.
JERRY BRIDGES

A Bible that's falling apart probably belongs to someone who isn't.
CHRISTIAN JOHNSON

❧

One who uses the Bible as his guide never loses his sense of direction.
AUTHOR UNKNOWN

❧

*It ain't those parts of the Bible that I can't understand that bother me,
it is the parts that I do understand.*
MARK TWAIN

❧

*No one ever graduates from Bible study
until he meets the author face-to-face.*
E. T. HARRIS

❧

*God the Father is the giver of Holy Scripture;
God the Son is the theme of Holy Scripture;
and God the Spirit is the author, authenticator,
and interpreter of Holy Scripture.*
J. I. PACKER

A GOSPEL-CENTERED LIFE

MEMORIZE THE GOSPEL

You might not think you're good at memorizing Scripture. That's okay. Don't give up. Work at it. God isn't keeping score. Even if it takes you longer than someone else, it's worth the effort.

PRAY THE GOSPEL

There's nothing complicated about this. To pray the gospel, simply begin by thanking God for the blessing of eternal life, purchased through the death of His Son. Acknowledge that Christ's work on the cross is what makes your very prayer possible.

SING THE GOSPEL

A Christian's heart should be brimming every day with the song of Calvary. This is another opportunity to be strategic. There are countless worship CDs available, but it's important to choose ones that draw our attention to the amazing truth of what God has done on our behalf.

REVIEW HOW THE GOSPEL
HAS CHANGED YOU

Many people today want to forget the past. The mistakes they've made and the sins they've committed aren't subjects they like to revisit. But for Christians, one of the best ways we can draw near the blazing fire of the cross is to remember the past. It should remind us of how marvelous God's salvation really is.

STUDY THE GOSPEL

Never be content with your current grasp of the gospel. The gospel is life-permeating, world-altering, universe-changing truth. It has more facets than any diamond. Its depths man will never exhaust.

C. J. MAHANEY
CONDENSED FROM "THE CROSS CENTERED LIFE"

APPLYING SCRIPTURE TO YOUR LIFE

- ❦ Realize that all Scripture is without error.

- ❦ Develop a daily and systematic reading program.

- ❦ Pray for Holy Spirit–led insights and dependence.

- ❦ Study what the author intended through insights from pastors.

- ❦ Memorize key passages.

- ❦ Meditate on meaning.

- ❦ Apply its commands.

- ❦ Claim its promises.

- ❦ Share it with others.

- ❦ Fall in love with its Author.

JOHN VAN DIEST
ASSOCIATE PUBLISHER

THE CLAIMS OF JESUS

Jesus claimed to be God in the flesh.

JOHN 5:17–18

Jesus claimed power to raise the dead.

JOHN 5:21

Jesus claimed to be the future judge of all men.

JOHN 5:22

Jesus claimed equal honor with God.

JOHN 5:23

Jesus claimed the authority to dispense eternal life.

JOHN 5:24

Jesus claimed to be the source of life.

JOHN 5:26–27

TIM LAHAYE
CONDENSED FROM "WHY BELIEVE IN JESUS?"

THE ABC'S OF GOD'S CHARACTER

Able; Available; Advocate

Beloved; Beauty; Bridegroom

Creator; Compassionate; Counselor

Deliverer; Defender; Delight

Eternal; Exalted; Everlasting

Faithful; Forgiving; Friend

Gentle; Giver; Guide

High Priest; Holy; Husband

Indwelling; Inviting; Infinite

Just; Joy; Jewel

Keeper; King; Kind

Light; Life; Love

Maker; Merciful; Majestic

Nourishment; Near; Nurturer

Owner; Omnipotent; Omniscient

Protector; Provider; Powerful

Quiet; Quick; Quotable

Refuge; Reward; Rock

Shepherd; Strength; Sufficiency

Teacher; Truth; Tender

Unchangeable; Understanding; Unconquerable

Victor; Virtuous; Vindicator

Wonderful Counselor; Worthy; Willing

X-tra Good! X-cellent! X-treme Love!

Yahweh; Yours; the Same Yesterday and Today

Zealous; Zestful; A to Z

CHERI FULLER
ADAPTED FROM "WHEN CHILDREN PRAY"

THE HOLY SPIRIT

HE SPEAKS.
"He who has an ear, let him hear what the Spirit says to the churches." (REVELATION 2:7)

HE INTERCEDES.
In the same way the Spirit also helps our weakness; for we do not know how to pray as we should, but the Spirit Himself intercedes for us with groanings too deep for words. (ROMANS 8:26)

HE TESTIFIES.
"When the Helper comes, whom I will send to you from the Father, that is the Spirit of truth who proceeds from the Father, He will testify about Me." (JOHN 15:26)

HE LEADS.
For all who are being led by the Spirit of God, these are sons of God. (ROMANS 8:14)

HE GUIDES.
"When He, the Spirit of truth, comes, he will guide you into all the truth." (JOHN 16:13)

HE APPOINTS.
Be on guard for yourselves and for all the flock, among which the Holy Spirit has made you overseers, to shepherd the church of God which He purchased with His own blood. (ACTS 20:28)

HE CAN BE LIED TO.

But Peter said, "Ananias, why has Satan filled your heart to lie to the Holy Spirit and to keep back some of the price of the land?" (ACTS 5:3)

HE CAN BE INSULTED.

How much severer punishment do you think he will deserve who has trampled under foot the Son of God...and has insulted the Spirit of grace? (HEBREWS 10:29)

HE CAN BE BLASPHEMED.

"Therefore I say to you, any sin and blasphemy shall be forgiven...but blasphemy against the Spirit shall not be forgiven." (MATTHEW 12:31)

HE CAN BE GRIEVED.

Do not grieve the Holy Spirit of God, by whom you were sealed for the day of redemption. (EPHESIANS 4:30)

BILLY GRAHAM
CONDENSED FROM "THE HOLY SPIRIT"
SCRIPTURE FROM NEW AMERICAN STANDARD BIBLE

TRUTHS ABOUT GOD

- God loves you unconditionally.

- God knows you completely.

- God listens to you intently.

- God forgives you willingly.

- God is with you constantly.

- God is too right to be wrong.

- God is majestically beautiful.

- God is perpetually good.

- God is marvelously wise.

- God never changes.

- God is incredibly patient.

- God is holy, righteous, and perfect.

- God is light and life.

~ God supplies all your needs.

~ God is eternally faithful.

~ God is infinitely powerful.

~ God never makes mistakes.

~ God has wonderful plans for you.

~ God desires your intimate friendship.

~ God always keeps his promises.

~ God is entirely just.

~ God is slow to anger.

~ God is exceedingly gracious.

~ God is full of mercy.

~ God is the giver of every good gift.

~ God is absolutely awesome.

LOREN FISCHER
PASTOR AND SEMINARY PROFESSOR

RESPONDING TO GOD'S WORD

I WILL...

- follow His Word
- obey His Word
- walk in His Word
- reflect His Word
- learn His Word
- hide His Word in my heart
- recite His Word aloud
- rejoice in His Word
- study His Word
- delight in His Word
- live His Word
- open my eyes to His Word
- desire His Word
- meditate on His Word
- know His Word
- cling to His Word
- put His Word into practice
- trust in His Word

- devote myself to His Word
- speak of His Word
- honor His Word
- love His Word
- be firmly anchored to His Word
- believe in His Word
- put my hope in His Word
- concentrate on His Word
- strain to see His Word
- never forget His Word
- keep my mind on His Word
- not turn from His Word
- understand His Word
- find joy in His Word
- think about His Word

PSALM 119
FROM THE NEW LIVING TRANSLATION

HOW GOD RESPONDS

When you CRY, He will COMFORT you.

When you are HAPPY, He will LAUGH with you.

When you need to TALK, He will LISTEN.

When you need DIRECTION, He will GUIDE.

When you are LONELY, He will be THERE.

When you are FRIGHTENED, He will PROTECT you.

When you need a FRIEND, He will CARE for you.

When you need HOPE, He will NEVER let you down.

DR. STEVE STEPHENS
AUTHOR AND SEMINAR SPEAKER

THE LAST WORDS OF CHRIST

"Father, forgive them, for they do not know what they are doing."
LUKE 23:34

To the thief on the cross,
"I tell you the truth, today you will be with me in paradise."
LUKE 23:43

To his mother and to John, the disciple,
"Dear woman, here is your son."
..."Here is your mother."
JOHN 19:26–27

"My God, my God, why have you forsaken me?"
MATTHEW 27:46

"I am thirsty."
JOHN 19:28

"It is finished."
JOHN 19:30

"Father, into your hands I commit my spirit."
LUKE 23:46

THE HOLY BIBLE

4
Worship And Praise

Giving adoration to the Lord of all

JUST GIVE ME JESUS

JESUS IS...

the Wind beneath my wings,

the Treasure I seek,

the Foundation on which I build,

the Song in my heart,

the Object of my desire,

the Breath of my life—

He is my All in all!

ANNE GRAHAM LOTZ
FROM "JUST GIVE ME JESUS"

SEVEN REASONS CHRIST
SUFFERED AND DIED

1.
TO ACHIEVE HIS OWN RESURRECTION FROM THE DEAD.

The wrath of God was satisfied with the suffering and death of Jesus. The holy curse against sin was fully absorbed. The price of forgiveness was totally paid. The righteousness of God was completely vindicated. All that was left to accomplish was the public declaration of God's endorsement. This He gave by raising Jesus from the dead.

2.
TO SHOW HIS OWN LOVE FOR US.

The sufferings and death of Christ have to do with me personally. It is *my* sin that cuts me off from God, not sin in general. I am lost and perishing; all I can do is plead for mercy. Then I see Christ suffering and dying, and I embrace the beauty and bounty of Christ as my treasure. And there flows into my heart this great reality—the love of Christ for *me*.

3.
IN ORDER TO CANCEL THE LEGAL DEMANDS
OF THE LAW AGAINST US.

There is no salvation by balancing records. There is only salvation by canceling records. The record of our bad deeds (including our defective good deeds), along with the just penalties that each deserves, must be blotted out—not balanced. This is what Christ suffered and died to accomplish.

4.
TO PROVIDE THE BASIS FOR OUR JUSTIFICATION
AND TO COMPLETE THE OBEDIENCE THAT BECOMES
OUR RIGHTEOUSNESS.

In the courtroom of God, we have not kept the law. Therefore, justification, in ordinary terms, is hopeless. Yes, amazingly, because of Christ, the Bible says God "justifies the ungodly" who trust in His grace. Christ fulfilled all righteousness perfectly; and then that righteousness was reckoned to be mine when I trusted in Him. Christ's death became the basis for our pardon *and* our perfection.

5.

TO OBTAIN FOR US ALL THINGS THAT ARE GOOD FOR US.

He will give us all things that are good for us. All things that we really need in order to be conformed to the image of His Son. All things we need in order to obtain everlasting joy. The suffering and death of Christ guarantee that God will give us all things that we need to do His will and to give Him glory and to attain everlasting love.

6.

TO BRING US TO GOD.

The evidence we have been changed is that we want the things that bring us to the enjoyment of God. This is the greatest thing Christ died for. We were made to experience full and lasting happiness from seeing and savoring the glory of God.

7.

TO GIVE US ETERNAL LIFE.

All that is good—all that will bring true and lasting happiness—will be preserved and purified and intensified. We will be changed so that we are capable of dimensions of happiness that were inconceivable to us in this life. For this Christ suffered and died. Why would we not embrace Him as our treasure?

JOHN PIPER
ADAPTED FROM "THE PASSION OF JESUS CHRIST"

NAMES OF JESUS

✝ Advocate ✝ All in All ✝ Alpha and Omega ✝ Ancient of Days

✝ Anointed One ✝ Arm of the Lord ✝ Atoning Sacrifice ✝ Banner

for the People ✝ Beloved ✝ Branch ✝ Bread of Life ✝ Bridegroom

✝ Bright Morning Star ✝ Carpenter ✝ Chief Cornerstone ✝ Christ

✝ Dayspring ✝ Door ✝ Everlasting Father ✝ Exact Representation

of His Being ✝ Faithful and True Witness ✝ Firstborn Over All

Creation ✝ Friend ✝ God ✝ Good Shepherd ✝ Head of the Church

✝ Heir of All Things ✝ High Priest ✝ Holy One ✝ Horn of Salvation

✝ I am ✝ Image of the Invisible God ✝ Immanuel ✝ Indescribable

Gift ✝ Judge ✝ King of Kings ✝ Lamb of God ✝ Leader and

Commander ✢ Life ✢ Light of the World ✢ Lily of the Valley ✢ Lion

of the Tribe of Judah ✢ Living One ✢ Living Water ✢ **Lord** ✢ Man

of Sorrows ✢ Mediator ✢ Messenger of Covenant ✢ **Mighty** God

✢ Only Begotten Son ✢ Our Hope ✢ Our Passover ✢ Overseer

✢ Pioneer of Our Faith ✢ Prince of Peace ✢ Prophet ✢ Physician

✢ Rabboni ✢ Radiance of God's Glory ✢ Ransom ✢ Redeemer ✢ The

Resurrection and the Life ✢ Rock ✢ Rose of Sharon ✢ Savior

✢ Scepter ✢ Servant ✢ Shiloh ✢ Son of David ✢ **Son** of Man

✢ Star ✢ Sun of Righteousness ✢ Teacher ✢ The True Vine

✢ TheTruth ✢ The Way ✢ Wonderful Counselor ✢ Word

HENRY GARIEPY
CONDENSED FROM "100 PORTRAITS OF CHRIST"

GOD IN SEVEN TRIBUTES

*In Psalm 18, King David used seven tributes
to describe and laud God:*

⚞ MY STRENGTH. The psalmist knew where his strength
lay—in God. Without God he would have succumbed;
with Him he was victorious.

⚞ MY ROCK. My cliff. When the storm beat the hardest, he
found God a rock, a solid rock, a cliff of shelter.

⚞ MY FORTRESS. A place of defense and protection. There is
no safety like Fort Divine.

⚞ MY DELIVERER. The original word is often translated
shield, a shield buckled to the arm. Life is a warfare, and to
win we need God on our arm when we raise it in defense.

⚞ THE HORN OF MY SALVATION. Jehovah was to the
writer what the horn is to an animal, the means of defense.

⚞ MY HIGH TOWER. Or refuge, that being the translation
of the word in Psalm 9:9. Truly, "The name of the LORD is
a strong tower; the righteous man runneth into it, and is
safe" (Proverbs 18:10, KJV).

How great God is!

⸎

LEROY BROWNLOW
FROM "A PSALM IN MY HEART"

THE AWESOME GOD

→ You are holy, the only one who does wonderful things.

→ You are strong; You are great; You are most high.

→ You are the almighty King, King of heaven and earth.

→ You are good, every good and the greatest good.

→ You are love; You are knowledge.

→ You are humility; You are patience.

→ You are every sufficient richness; You are beauty.

→ You are protector, guardian, and defender.

→ You are our faith; You are our hope.

→ You are our amazing sweetness.

→ You are our eternal life.

→ You are awesome Lord, all-powerful God, merciful Savior.

CONDENSED FROM FRANCIS OF ASSISI
FOUNDER OF THE ORDER OF FRANCISCANS

RESPONDING TO GOD'S GLORY

✝ HONOR HIS GLORY

Focus on His Word and live in a way that brings Him pleasure.

✝ DECLARE HIS GLORY

Tell others about the awesomeness of God
and about every good gift that comes from Him.

✝ PRAISE HIS GLORY

Express joy and thankfulness to God through prayer,
music, and other expressions of worship.

✝ REFLECT HIS GLORY

Respond to the highs and lows of life with love,
patience, and grace—thereby showing the world
a small glimpse of God's character.

✝ REVERE HIS GLORY

Acknowledge God's ultimate majesty with a genuine
display of awe, respect, and humility.

✝ BE FILLED BY HIS GLORY

Allow God's love to control, transform,
and overflow in every area of life.

JOHN VAN DIEST
ASSOCIATE PUBLISHER

HONORING GOD'S HOLINESS

∞

HONOR GOD'S NAME.

God's name reflects His character. There's nothing wrong, impure, dirty, sly, or underhanded in Him. He is perfect. His Son, Jesus, lived a sinless, holy life. We acknowledge God's holiness when we use His name with proper respect.

∞

HONOR GOD'S WORD.

It's called the Holy Bible for a reason. Every word in it is from God; each story is true. Because God is holy, His words are holy. That's why we treat our Bibles with care.

∞

KEEP THE SABBATH HOLY.

Christians should model this behavior by attending church and remembering why God set aside a day of rest. He took six days to make the heavens and earth and rested when it was done. He set aside a day each week for us to rest and thank Him for all He has done. It's a day to praise and honor Him, to enjoy Him in the midst of family and friends.

DEAN RIDINGS
ADAPTED FROM "FOCUS ON THE FAMILY" MAGAZINE

ACTS OF WORSHIP

Worship does not need an occasion or a reason.
It is spontaneous and happens as the overflow
of a loving and grateful heart.
LYNDA HUNTER BJORKLUND

❧

We are often so caught up in our activities
that we tend to worship our work, work at our play,
and play at our worship.
CHUCK SWINDOLL

❧

Worship renews the spirit as sleep renews the body.
RICHARD CLARKE CABOT

❧

Worship is…
A renewed reverence for God,
A practice of the presence of God,
A deepened sense of the community of God.
RON ALLEN AND GORDON BORROR

Worship is far more than praising, singing, and praying to God.
Worship is a lifestyle of enjoying God, loving Him,
and giving ourselves to be used for His purposes.

RICK WARREN

I find that my worship is richer
when I offer the Lord praise and thanks for three things:
who He is, what He does, and what He gives.

RUTH MYERS

"Worthy is the Lamb that was slain
to receive power
and riches
and wisdom
and might
and honor
and glory
and blessing."

REVELATION 5:12, NASB

THE IMPORTANCE OF PRAISE

→ Praise strengthens your faith.

→ Praise tunes in God's enriching presence.

→ Praise activates God's power.

→ Praise helps you profit more from your trials.

→ Praise helps you experience Christ in your life.

→ Praise helps you demonstrate God's reality.

→ Praise helps you overcome Satan and his strategies.

→ Praise brings glory and pleasure to God.

RUTH MYERS
FROM "31 DAYS OF PRAISE"

PRAISE CHANGES US

PRAISE CHANGES OUR ATTITUDE
You cannot harbor anger, bitterness, resentment, or hatred toward others and genuinely praise God at the same time.

PRAISE CHANGES OUR ENERGY LEVEL
There is a special strength that is imparted to those who praise the Lord. This kind of strength gives us the power to endure, to persevere, to outlast the bad times.

PRAISE CHANGES OUR RELATIONSHIPS
It's very difficult to remain at odds with a person over temporary human differences when you find yourself in agreement about the goodness and greatness of God.

PRAISE CHANGES OUR SPIRITUAL PERCEPTIONS
Praise opens our eyes and ears to God. When we focus on Him in praise, we are much more likely to hear what He has to say to us.

PRAISE CHANGES OUR DESIRES
There is a huge difference in desires that are subjected first to a hearty dose of praise.

MICHAEL YOUSSEF
CONDENSED FROM "EMPOWERED BY PRAISE"

DAILY WORSHIP

The fifth Psalm contains an excellent plan for living:

MEDITATION: "Consider my meditation." One of the grievous errors of this age is our fast pace, which leaves no time to think and meditate. Meditating on the majesty of God will make a difference in our lives.

MORNING PRAYER: "In the morning will I direct my prayer unto thee." A good way to start the day. God's help is needed every day, all day.

ACCEPTANCE OF MERCY: "I will come into thy house in the multitude of thy mercy." We are imperfect. Mercy is needed. And if we accept God's mercy, which forgives us, then we should forgive ourselves and put our mistakes behind us.

WORSHIP: "And in thy fear will I worship." Approach God with reverential fear. He is God. We are human. Never try to humanize Him. Keep the distinction. Let God be God. Worship Him. The need is as old as man.

A STRAIGHT WAY: "Make thy way straight before my face"—not smooth, not easy. Just let the way be Thine and show me clearly.

REJOICE: "But let all those that put their trust in thee rejoice." Our days should be lived joyfully—not in serving a rigorous sentence. And where does it come from? From trusting the One who created us for joyful living.

LEROY BROWNLOW
CONDENSED FROM "A PSALM IN MY HEART"
SCRIPTURES ARE FROM THE KING JAMES VERSION

BLESS YOU, LORD...

- For not abandoning me when I abandoned You.

- For offering Your hand of love in my darkest, most lonely moment.

- For putting up with such a stubborn soul as mine.

- For loving me more than I love myself.

- For continuing to pour out Your blessings upon me, even though I respond so poorly.

- For repaying my sin with Your love.

- For being constant and unchanging, amidst all the changes of the world.

- For Your countless blessings on me and on all Your creatures.

TERESA OF AVILA
AUTHOR OF "THE INTERIOR CASTLE"

A HEART OF THANKSGIVING

THANKFULNESS
acknowledges that God is our provider.

THANKFULNESS
prevents a complaining spirit.

THANKFULNESS
creates a positive outlook on life.

THANKFULNESS
invites joy to dwell in our hearts.

KENT CROCKETT
FROM "MAKING TODAY COUNT FOR ETERNITY"

HOW TO PRESS C-L-O-S-E-R TO GOD

COME TO HIM

The King of kings, the Lord of lords, the One whose name is above every other name has invited you to spend time with Him. He wants to listen, to comfort, to help. Let His words connect with your longings: "Come to me, all of you who are weary and carry heavy burdens, and I will give you rest." When you come to Him, you are beginning to press closer.

LEAN ON HIM

Who do you lean on when things get rough? The Lord is good for leaning. He is strong and steady. He will never leave you or forsake you. He has called you by name and made you His. When you pass through the deep waters, He has promised to be with you. When you lean on Him, you are pressing closer.

OPEN YOUR BIBLE

God wants his Word to be an oasis for your soul. He has filled it with comfort verses that fit your heartbreak. The Psalms especially speak words of comfort, but there are many other verses that will be precious to you. When you open God's love letter, you are pressing closer.

Surrender

I sometimes doubt God because I don't think He is working things out *my* way or on *my* time schedule. Surrendering means trusting *God's* way and *God's* time schedule. When you surrender, you are pressing closer.

Eternalize

Try to find God's perspective for your circumstances. It is a relief to cling to what we know as absolute truth. There is a God and He loves us. Even when life is not always fair, God is. Even better, He's merciful! One day He will return and make all the wrongs right. When you are looking at things through an eternal perspective, it's easier to press closer.

Release

Release means giving everything to God. It means packing up all the worry, all the *what ifs*, all the doubts, all the debris from our shattered dreams and giving them to Him. When you release your sorrow and disappointment to God, you have pressed closer.

ALICE GRAY
CONDENSED FROM "THE WORN OUT WOMAN"

THE PURPOSE OF WORSHIP

⊰ WORSHIP CREATES CHRISTIAN COMMUNITY

In worship we are drawn closer to one another, are encouraged, taught, accepted, loved, and inspired by one another. We are reminded that though we may come from different economic, educational, social, ethnic, and racial backgrounds, we are all one in Jesus Christ.

⊰ WORSHIP CELEBRATES THE GOODNESS OF GOD

Worship is a joyful celebration of God's salvation and deliverance. It is for celebrating the goodness and grace of God, what He has done in the past, and what He is doing right now. But most of all, each of us can celebrate being delivered from the hand of spiritual and eternal death. God has set us free!

⊰ GOD IS THE CENTER OF ALL WORSHIP

God is the center of worship because He is worthy of all the praise and the honor. The Lord is a great God and a great King above all gods. Beside Him there is none other. He is God over all the creation and He is the Ruler of the entire cosmos. In worship I am filled with the Holy Spirit. In worship I see God.

REV. DR. GEOFFREY V. GUNS
SELECTED FROM HIS SERMON ON PSALM 95:1–7

5
Prayer

Lifting your heart and soul

HE IS ABLE

> He is able to *do,*
>> for He is neither idle, nor inactive, nor dead.

> He is able to do what we *ask,*
>> for He hears and answers prayer.

> He is able to do what we ask *or think,*
>> for He reads our thoughts.

> He is able to do *all* that we ask or think,
>> for He knows it all and can perform it all.

> He is able to do *more than* all we ask or think,
>> for His expectations are higher than ours.

> He is able to do *much more abundantly* than all that
> we ask or think,
>> for He does not give His grace by calculated measure.

> He is able to do *far more abundantly* than all that
> we ask or think,
>> for He is a God of superabundance.

C. SAMUEL STORMS
FROM "GRANDEUR OF GOD"
BASED ON EPHESIANS 3:20

WHY PRAY?

WE ARE COMMANDED TO PRAY.

For example, Jesus said we are to pray at all times and "not to lose heart" (Luke 18:1), and we are told to "pray without ceasing" (1 Thessalonians 5:17). Prayer should define our lives.

THROUGH PRAYER WE MEET WITH GOD AND EXPERIENCE A RELATIONSHIP WITH HIM.

What an unspeakable honor to come boldly into the presence of the Creator of the universe! One vehicle for this is praise. The Scriptures tell us that God inhabits the praises of His people (see Psalm 22:3).

IN PRAYER WE HAVE THE OPPORTUNITY TO CONFESS AND REPENT OF OUR SINS TO GOD AND HAVE A CLEAN CONSCIENCE.

In 1 John 1:9 we are told, "If we confess our sins, He is faithful and righteous to forgive us our sins and to cleanse us from all unrighteousness."

PRAYER IS THE WAY WE RECEIVE ANSWERS
AND WISDOM FROM THE LORD.

"You do not have because you do not ask" (James 4:2). In James 1:5 we also discover that prayer reveals God's wisdom to us. God delights in giving us the insights we need to handle the problems we face in life.

PRAYER WILL LIGHTEN OUR LOAD.

In Matthew 11:28, Jesus said, "Come to Me, all who are weary and heavy-laden, and I will give you rest." Prayer is a practical way to exchange our worries for His peace. "Be anxious for nothing, but in everything by prayer and supplication with thanksgiving let your requests be made known to God. And the peace of God, which surpasses all comprehension, will guard your hearts and your minds in Christ Jesus" (Philippians 4:6–7).

DENNIS AND BARBARA RAINEY
ADAPTED FROM "TWO HEARTS PRAYING AS ONE"
SCRIPTURES ARE FROM THE NEW AMERICAN STANDARD BIBLE

HOW TO PRAY

PRAY FROM SCRIPTURE

for then your thoughts will be centered on God's thoughts and promises.

PRAY IN YOUR SANCTUARY

for then you can quiet your spirit to enter into His presence and focus on Him.

PRAY WITH THANKSGIVING AND WORSHIP OF GOD

There is no better way to establish a sense of faith and hope in your prayers. And you will find no better example of such praying than in the Psalms.

PRAY HONESTLY

God knows your heart. He isn't freaked out by what He sees there. He loves you, and He looks for those who are honest before Him.

PRAY SPECIFICALLY

Make your specific request known to Him; this is His command.

PRAY PERSISTENTLY

If your heart has a particular burden, don't give up. Give the Lord time to accomplish His good purposes. He hears your prayers, and His timing is always best. "He who comes to God must believe that He is and that He is a rewarder of those who seek Him" (Hebrews 11:6, NASB).

PRAY WHEN YOU AWAKEN AND WHEN YOU FALL TO SLEEP

When you open your eyes in the morning, you greet the Lord. When you close them to sleep at night, you thank Him for another day.
.

PRAY AS YOU GO ABOUT LIVING YOUR LIFE

The brilliant writer G. K. Chesterton said: "You say grace before meals. But I say grace before the concert and the opera, and grace before the play and pantomime, and grace before I open a book, and grace before sketching, painting, swimming, fencing, and grace before I dip the pen in ink."

PRAY IN CRISIS

Crisis praying is when you pull out all the stops. You stop whatever you're doing and pray fervently. You seek His face regarding some deep crisis or a huge decision in your life.

STEVE AND MARY FARRAR
ADAPTED FROM "OVERCOMING OVERLOAD"

QUESTIONS TO ASK BEFORE PRAYING

Before bringing a request to the Lord, ask:
If God granted this request...

WOULD IT BRING GLORY TO HIM?

❦

WOULD IT ADVANCE HIS KINGDOM?

❦

WOULD IT HELP PEOPLE?

❦

WOULD IT HELP ME TO GROW SPIRITUALLY?

BILL HYBELS
FROM "TOO BUSY NOT TO PRAY"

FOUR WAYS GOD ANSWERS PRAYER

If the request is wrong,
God says, *No.*

If the timing is wrong,
God says, *Slow.*

If you are wrong,
God says, *Grow.*

But if the request is right,
the timing is right
and you are right,
God says, *Go.*

AUTHOR UNKNOWN
FROM "TOO BUSY NOT TO PRAY"

SIX REASONS FOR UNANSWERED PRAYER

1.
PRAYERLESSNESS
You do not have, because you do not ask God.

ISAIAH 4:2

2.
UNCONFESSED SIN
*Your iniquities have separated you from your God;
your sins have hidden his face from you,
so that he will not hear.*

ISAIAH 59:2

3.
UNRESOLVED RELATIONAL CONFLICT
*If you are offering your gift at the altar and there remember
that your brother has something against you, leave your gift
there in front of the altar. First go and be reconciled to your
brother; then come and offer your gift.*

MATTHEW 5:23–24

4.
SELFISHNESS
*When you ask, you do not receive,
because you ask with wrong motives,
that you may spend what you get on your pleasures.*

JAMES 4:3

5.
UNCARING ATTITUDE
If you close your ear to the cry of the poor,
you will cry out and not be heard.

PROVERBS 21:13, NRSV

6.
INADEQUATE FAITH
If any of you lacks wisdom, he should ask God,
who gives generously to all without finding fault,
and it will be given to him.
But when he asks, he must believe and not doubt,
because he who doubts is like a wave of the sea,
blown and tossed by the wind.
That man should not think he will
receive anything from the Lord.

JAMES 1:5–7

BILL HYBELS
FROM "TOO BUSY NOT TO PRAY"

TOUCHPOINTS

ACKNOWLEDGMENT
Our Father in heaven

REVERENCE
Hallowed be your name

ANTICIPATION
Your kingdom come

SUBMISSION
Your will be done

PETITION
Give us today our daily bread

CONFESSION
Forgive us our debts

GRACE
As we also have forgiven our debtors

GUIDANCE
And lead us not into temptation

PROTECTION
But deliver us from the evil one

PRAISE
For yours is the kingdom and the power and the glory forever.

JESUS
MATTHEW 6:9–13

FIVE-FINGER PRAYER

1.

YOUR THUMB IS NEAREST TO YOU.

So begin your prayers by praying for those closest to you. They are the easiest to remember. To pray for our loved ones is, as C. S. Lewis said, a "sweet duty."

2.

THE NEXT FINGER IS THE POINTING FINGER.

Pray for those who heal, teach, and instruct. This includes doctors, teachers, and ministers. They need wisdom in pointing others in the right direction.

3.

THE NEXT FINGER IS THE TALLEST FINGER.

It reminds us of our leaders. Pray for the president and leaders in business and industry. These people shape our nation. They need God's guidance.

4.

THE FOURTH FINGER IS THE RING FINGER.

This is our weakest finger. It reminds us to pray for the weak, those in trouble or in pain. You cannot pray enough for them.

5.

AND LAST COMES OUR LITTLE FINGER, THE SMALLEST FINGER OF ALL.

This is where we should place ourselves in relation to God and others. The Bible says, "He who is least among you all—he is the greatest" (Luke 9:48). After you've prayed for the other four groups, your own needs will be put into perspective.

AUTHOR UNKNOWN

WHAT HAPPENS WHEN WE PRAY

⚜ WE MATURE

We gain faith and grow in our understanding of Him.

⚜ WE ARE HUMBLED

We are reminded that He is great and
we are not; He is holy and we are
not; He is all-wise and we are not.

⚜ WE ARE BLESSED

God meets the needs we have laid
before Him.

STEVE AND MARY FARRAR
FROM "OVERCOMING OVERLOAD"

WAYS TO PRAY

† Pray humbly.

† Pray boldly, persisting in faith.

† Pray continually.

† Pray in faith for your need.

† Pray for others.

† Pray with praise.

† Pray in His name and will.

† Pray to receive.

† Pray with another in agreement.

DR. LARRY KEEFAUVER
FROM "WHEN GOD DOESN'T HEAL NOW"

WHAT PRAYER PROVIDES

PROTECTION
Keep me safe, O God, for I have come to you for refuge.

PSALM 16:1

PURPOSE
Be glad for all God is planning for you.
Be patient in trouble, and always be prayerful.

ROMANS 12:12

POWER
I pray that you will begin to understand the incredible
greatness of his power for us who believe him.

EPHESIANS 1:19

PROVISION
Don't worry about anything; instead, pray about everything.
Tell God what you need, and thank him for all he has done.

PHILIPPIANS 4:6

PEACE
I cried out to the LORD, and he answered me from his holy
mountain. I lay down and slept, I woke up in safety, for the
LORD was watching over me.

PSALM 3:4-5

PERSPECTIVE
Always be joyful.
Keep on praying, no matter what happens,
always be thankful.

1 THESSALONIANS 5:16-18

PASSION
The end of the world is coming soon.
Therefore, be earnest and disciplined in your prayers.

1 PETER 4:7

PURITY
Create in me a clean heart, O God.
Renew a right spirit within me.

PSALM 51:10

JOHN VAN DIEST
ASSOCIATE PUBLISHER
SCRIPTURE FROM NEW LIVING TRANSLATION

REACHING UP

PRAY
while God listens.

HEAR
while God speaks.

BELIEVE
while God promises.

OBEY
while God commands.

JOHN MASON
POET AND HYMN WRITER

TRUE PRAYER IS...

An inventory of needs

A catalog of necessities

An exposure of secret wounds

A revelation of hidden poverty

CHARLES SPURGEON
PREACHER AND THEOLOGIAN

THE ABC'S OF PRAYER

Adore God's awesomeness

Believe in God

Confess to God

Dwell on God's beauty

Express your heart

Find time

Give thanks for all things

Humble yourself

Invite others to join you

Joyfully go to God

Keep a prayer journal

Listen to God

Meditate on God's greatness

Notice the needs of others

Open your heart

Push away distractions

Quietly reflect on God's goodness

Rest in God's wisdom

Submit to God's will

Trust in God's faithfulness

Unceasingly seek God

Visit God's house

Worship God

e**X**perience God's love

Yield to God

Zealously pursue God

DUSTY, DYLAN, AND BRITTANY STEPHENS
AGES 10 THROUGH 15

CRYING OUT TO GOD

FOR POWER IN HOLY AND RIGHTEOUS LIVING

David says, "In the day when I *cried out,* you answered me, and made me bold with strength in my soul" (Psalm 138:3). God wants us to cry out to Him for the strength of soul available through His Spirit to break the bonds of unrighteousness in our lives.

FOR WISDOM

In the book of Proverbs we're told to "*cry out* for discernment, and *lift up your voice* for understanding" (2:3). When we ask for wisdom He will place things on our mind which are amazing.

FOR FAITH

"Immediately the father of the child cried out and said with tears, 'Lord, I believe; help my unbelief!'" (Mark 9:24). Our effective cry to the Lord can lead to a major lesson in faith not only for ourselves, but also for those around us.

FOR SPIRITUAL VICTORY

By crying out to God and asking Him to overcome evil's power, we seek the victory only He can provide, because He is over all the dark forces and powers which represent our true enemy. "For we do not wrestle against flesh and blood, but against principalities, against powers, against the rulers of the darkness of this age, against spiritual hosts of wickedness in the heavenly places" (Ephesians 6:12).

FOR BLESSING

It is certainly proper to cry out to God to bless us. While wrestling with the angel of God, Jacob said, "I will not let You go unless You bless me!" (Genesis 32:26). In the crying out for blessing, Jacob had power with God.

FOR HEALING

In the book of Exodus, it was after Moses cried out to the Lord for the people's physical welfare that God promised them, "I am the LORD who heals you" (Exodus 15:26). The God of all compassion indeed hears our cry to be healed of affliction, both physical and spiritual.

FOR QUENCHING OUR SPIRITUAL THIRST

In our soul-thirst, we'll cry out for inner filling, and the Holy Spirit will draw our inward attention to the One "who Himself bore our sins in His own body on the tree, that we, having died to sins, might live for righteousness" (1 Peter 2:24). Then our eyes of faith will see that Christ is our all and our everything, the source and supply of our every satisfaction in time of need.

FOR OTHERS

"Samuel cried out to the LORD for Israel, and the LORD answered him" (1 Samuel 7:9). Our crying out is effective on behalf of others as well as for ourselves, as many have learned.

BILL GOTHARD
CONDENSED FROM "THE POWER OF CRYING OUT"
SCRIPTURE FROM NEW KING JAMES VERSION

PRAY FOR YOUR CHILDREN

Pray that your children will...

➤ fear the Lord and serve Him.
➤ know Christ as Savior early in life.
➤ hate sin.
➤ be caught when they're guilty.
➤ have a responsible attitude in all their interpersonal relationships.
➤ respect those in authority over them.
➤ desire the right kind of friends and be protected from the wrong kind.
➤ be kept from the wrong mate and saved for the right one.
➤ be kept pure until marriage.
➤ learn to submit totally to God and actively resist Satan in all circumstances.
➤ be single-hearted, willing to be sold out to Jesus.
➤ be hedged in so they cannot find their way to wrong people or wrong places, and that wrong people cannot find their way to your children.
➤ have quick, repentant hearts.
➤ honor their parents so all will go well with them.
➤ be teachable and able to take correction.
➤ bear the fruit of the Spirit.
➤ live by the Spirit and not gratify their flesh.
➤ trust in the Lord for direction in every area of their lives.

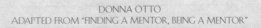

DONNA OTTO
ADAPTED FROM "FINDING A MENTOR, BEING A MENTOR"

6
Marriage

Appreciating life together

BUILDING A MARRIAGE OF FAITH

COMMITMENT 1
I commit to personally grow in Christ for the rest of my life.
Drawing closer to God in your marriage begins with your
personal relationship with Him alone.

COMMITMENT 2
I commit to our marriage for life and to
work to solve all problems that arise.
Problems come, but when you face them with the goal and
confidence of resolution, you can grow closer together in the process.

COMMITMENT 3
I commit to be faithful to my spouse in both mind and action.
Trust develops and problems are avoided when you decide,
"My spouse is the only one I will allow myself to
think about in this way."

COMMITMENT 4
I commit to communicate—no matter what.
Even when you'd rather do anything else,
decide when and how you will talk through difficult issues.

COMMITMENT 5
I commit to be a servant to my spouse.
Be willing to serve each other in thoughts and actions that
promote mutual dependence and appreciation.

CHARLES SWINDOLL
FROM "INSIGHTS" NEWSLETTER

PRAYING FOR YOUR WIFE

✝ HER SPIRIT

Lord…help her to stay focused on You, no matter how great the storm around her, so that she never strays off the path You have for her.

✝ HER EMOTIONS

Lord…heal her brokenheartedness and bind up her wounds. Make her secure in Your love and mine. Take away all fear, doubt, and discouragement, and give her clarity, joy, and peace.

✝ HER MARRIAGE

Lord…show me how to love my wife in an ever-deepening way that she can clearly perceive…protect our marriage…may we never waver in our commitment and devotion to You and to one another…

✝ HER RELATIONSHIPS

Lord… (give her) good, strong, healthy relationships with godly women…make my wife a light to her family, friends, coworkers, and community…

✝ HER SEXUALITY

Lord…teach us to show affection to one another in ways that keep romance and desire alive between us.

† HER FEARS

Lord…remind her to bring all her concerns to You in prayer so that Your peace that passes all understanding will permanently reside in her heart.

† HER PURPOSE

Lord…give her a sense of Your call on her life, and open doors of opportunity for her to develop and use her gifts in that calling.

† HER TRUST

Lord…make me always worthy of her trust…in any place where we have broken trust with one another, help us to reestablish it as strong. May we both trust You…

† HER PROTECTION

Lord…keep her safe from any accidents, diseases, or evil influences. Protect her in cars, planes, or wherever she is. Keep her out of harm's way.

† HER DESIRES

Lord…fulfill her deepest desires…I pray that the desires of our hearts will be perfectly knitted together. May we not only be caught up in our own dreams but in each other's as well.

STORMIE OMARTIAN
CONDENSED FROM "THE POWER OF A PRAYING HUSBAND"

MARRIAGE

PRAYING FOR YOUR HUSBAND

† HIS WORK

Lord…bless the work of my husband's hands. May his labor bring not only favor, success, and prosperity, but great fulfillment as well.

† HIS TEMPTATIONS

Lord…strengthen my husband to resist any temptation that comes his way…establish a wall of protection around him. Fill him with Your spirit, and flush out all that is not of You.

† HIS AFFECTION

Lord…enable each of us to lay aside self-consciousness or apathy and be effusive in our display of love. Help us to demonstrate how much we care for and value each other.

† HIS CHOICES

Lord…give him wisdom for every decision he makes. Help him to make godly choices and keep him from doing anything foolish.

† HIS HEALTH

Lord…make every part of his body function the way you designed it to…heal him of any disease, illness, injury, infirmity, or weakness. Strengthen his body…

† HIS INTEGRITY

Lord…make my husband a man of integrity, according to Your standards, and give him strength to say "yes" when he should say "yes" and courage to say "no" when he should say "no."

✝ HIS PRIORITIES

Lord...speak to him about making Your Word, prayer, and praise a priority. Enable him to place me and our children in greater prominence in his heart than career, friends, and activities.

✝ HIS ATTITUDE

Lord...give him a spirit of joy and keep him from growing into a grumpy old man. Help him to be anxious about nothing, but give thanks in all things so he can know the peace that passes all understanding.

✝ HIS FAITH

Lord...enlarge his ability to believe in You, Your Word, Your promises, Your ways, and Your power...may he seek You, rely totally upon You...and acknowledge You in everything he does.

✝ HIS FUTURE

Lord...give him a vision for his future. Help him to understand that Your plans for him are good...help him to mature and grow in You daily...

STORMIE OMARTIAN
CONDENSED FROM "THE POWER OF A PRAYING WIFE"

HOW TO LOVE YOUR WIFE

1. Prefer her over yourself.

2. Show interest in her interests.

3. Encourage her with words of appreciation.

4. Brighten her day with an unexpected card, note, flowers, or gift.

5. Listen with interest to her concerns while showing compassion.

6. Help her when she looks as if she needs it (don't wait to be asked!).

7. Do chivalrous things to let her know how special she is to you.

8. Give her nonsexual affection.

9. Seek to please and satisfy her during sexual intimacy.

10. Pray with her and lead her spiritually.

STUART SCOTT
ADAPTED FROM "THE EXEMPLARY HUSBAND"

HOW TO LOVE YOUR HUSBAND

1. Pray for him daily.

2. Speak words of kindness.

3. Give him an unexpected gift.

4. Thank him for something good he has done.

5. Praise him for one of his good character qualities.

6. Be humble enough to confess your own failures.

7. Reaffirm your commitment to him.

8. Initiate a special time of lovemaking with him.

9. Spend time with him doing something he likes to do.

10. Obey God and let your husband see Christ in you.

MARTHA PEACE
CONDENSED FROM "THE EXCELLENT WIFE"

I PROMISE THAT...

I will always love you.

After God, you will always be my first priority.

I am forever committed to this relationship
and will always work on this marriage.

I will always forgive you and work through conflicts.

I will always be faithful to you.

I will always be truthful with you.

I will always be there for you.

~～⌒

FRED LOWERY
FROM "COVENANT MARRIAGE"

NO MATTER WHAT HAPPENS

If things get better for us,
I WILL LOVE YOU.

If things get worse,
I WILL LOVE YOU.

If we get rich beyond our wildest dreams,
I WILL LOVE YOU.

If we grow poorer and don't own much,
I WILL LOVE YOU.

If you get sick,
I WILL LOVE YOU.

If you remain healthy,
I WILL LOVE YOU.

In fact, no matter what happens,
I WILL ALWAYS LOVE YOU.

GARY AND BARBARA ROSBERG
FROM "SERVING LOVE"

10 THINGS EVERY WIFE NEEDS TO KNOW

1. I need you to share your dreams, desires, and needs clearly—I'm not a mind reader.

2. I need you to be strong in your faith—it encourages me spiritually to lead.

3. I need you to pray for me—being a husband and father is a big responsibility.

4. Help me to develop spiritual partnerships with other men.

5. Give a good report about me to others—it encourages me to grow.

6. I value your acknowledgment of what I do around the house—it provides me energy to do more.

7. I enjoy conversation, but I need quiet time to reflect on my day. Then I can discuss it more easily.

8. I need your support when I take the lead in decision making. Help me consider all your input and other factors, and then give me room to think.

9. I need you to be my best friend. Oh, and one more…

10. Love me…all the time.

DAN MCAULEY
COLLEGE PROFESSOR AND MARRIAGE MENTOR

EIGHT THINGS EVERY HUSBAND NEEDS TO KNOW

1. Your wife needs you to be the spiritual leader of your home.

2. Your wife needs you to be her teammate in raising the kids and taking care of the home.

3. Your wife needs you to treat her like a princess.

4. Your wife needs you to communicate with her.

5. Your wife needs her friends and needs you to allow her time with the girls, but ultimately she wants you to be her best friend.

6. Your wife needs you to be a "triple A" encourager by giving her appreciation, affirmation, and admiration.

7. Your wife needs to feel emotionally filled before she desires to be sexually involved.

8. Your wife needs you to understand that there are some things you will never understand. This doesn't make either of you right or wrong—just different.

LISA TERKEURST
FROM "CAPTURE HER HEART"

THE PROVERBS 31 MARRIAGE...

For Wives

CULTIVATING TRUST

The excellent wife understands that a good marriage is founded on trust. She doesn't hurt, hinder, or discourage her husband.

PURSUING DREAMS

The excellent wife helps her husband and children realize their dreams, but she does not neglect the dreams and longings God has placed in her own heart.

NURTURING RELATIONSHIPS

The excellent wife gets up early or stays up late so she can generously share her gifts and hospitality with those God places in her life.

DEEPENING BEAUTY

The excellent wife nurtures an uplifting attitude, positive words, and kind actions. She realizes that pleasing God will give her true and lasting beauty.

RENÉE SANFORD
BIBLE TEACHER AND SEMINAR SPEAKER

THE PROVERBS 31 MARRIAGE...

For Husbands

CHERISHING

The good husband recognizes the true value of his wife. He sees her as one of God's priceless treasures and faithfully cares for her needs.

SUPPORTING

The good husband believes in the potential of his wife. He doesn't hold her back or put her down but encourages her to be productive and fulfilled.

LISTENING

The good husband realizes the importance of listening to and learning from his wife. His responses are kind, gentle, respectful, and truthful.

PRAISING

The good husband praises his wife for her virtues, godly character, endeavors, and accomplishments. He lets others know she is a treasure "far above jewels."

DAVID SANFORD
AUTHOR AND SEMINAR SPEAKER

HOW PRAYING TOGETHER CAN
HELP YOUR MARRIAGE

→ *Are you lacking intimacy in your marriage?* Praying together will take you to new levels of intimacy far beyond what you thought possible.

→ *Is there conflict in your marriage?* Praying together will defuse, disarm, resolve, and prevent disagreements.

→ *Do you want more transparency in your marriage?* Praying together is certain to open your hearts to one another.

→ *Do you feel distant from God?* Here's a scriptural promise to grab onto and apply: "Call to Me and I will answer you, and I will tell you great and might things, which you do not know" (Jeremiah 33:3).

→ *Are you fearful? Disappointed? Discouraged? Worried? Angry? Hopeless?* Praying together will calm the storms in your heart, marriage, and family.

→ *Are you struggling against sin?* Praying as a couple exposes sin so God can work.

→ *Are you near divorce?* Praying as a couple restores unity of heart, mind, and purpose.

DENNIS AND BARBARA RAINEY
FROM "TWO HEARTS PRAYING AS ONE"
SCRIPTURE IS FROM NEW AMERICAN STANDARD BIBLE

SIX STEPS FOR HANDLING CONFLICT

1.

Change what can be altered.

2.

Explain what can be understood.

3.

Teach what can be learned.

4.

Revise what can be improved.

5.

Negotiate what is open to compromise.

6.

Accept the rest.

DR. JAMES AND SHIRLEY DOBSON
FROM "NIGHT LIGHT"

WHEN YOUR LOVED ONE DOESN'T LOVE GOD

LIVE IN THE NOW.
Accept your relationship for what it is, and concentrate on cultivating peace and happiness. Instead of striving to alter your circumstances, set your mind on enjoying your life. Find what's good now and build on it.

∽

LIVE YOUR FAITH WITH INTEGRITY.
Let your spouse see that genuine Christianity isn't blind allegiance to a set of rigid standards, but a process of growth and change.

∽

LET YOUR ACTIONS SPEAK.
The loudest form of evangelism is a life that's changed. One man who is now a believer told me that his wife was always kind when he was harsh with her, and that drove him crazy. "I knew it was Jesus that kept her from blowing up at me."

∽

FIND COMMON GROUND AND HAVE FUN TOGETHER.
My friend makes a list of things she and her husband enjoy: swimming, watching Star Trek movies, vintage cars, and sex.

PRAY HARD.

Prayer is our link to God's presence, power, wisdom, and comfort. You might pray for conviction of sin and godly sorrow that leads to repentance (2 Corinthians 7:10); that God will take a spouse's heart of stone and replace it with a heart of flesh (Ezekiel 36:26); wisdom, courage, discernment, and opportunities to speak.

CULTIVATE YOUR FRIENDSHIP WITH CHRIST.

It's crucial to maintain Christian fellowship, Bible reading, and prayer. If you can, join a small group, and have them pray with you for your unsaved mate.

DON'T GIVE UP HOPE.

God knows what He's doing, and He knows those who are His (2 Timothy 2:19). Trust that He will do what's best for you and your spouse. We have this hope: "[God] is patient with you, not wanting anyone to perish, but everyone to come to repentance" (2 Peter 3:9). That means there's hope for your spouse—and hope for mine.

NANCY KENNEDY
CONDENSED FROM "MARRIAGE PARTNERSHIP" MAGAZINE

7
Family

Caring for one another

10 PURPOSES OF PARENTING

1. To model Jesus.

2. To pray for our children daily.

3. To demonstrate a life of integrity.

4. To set safe and appropriate boundaries.

5. To be a student of our children's world.

6. To promote our children's unique interests.

7. To encourage a passionate desire for truth.

8. To respect their abilities and self-determination.

9. To influence their beliefs, rather than control their behaviors.

10. To shape their environment, because it will influence their hearts.

DAVID SEEL JR.
FROM "PARENTING WITHOUT PERFECTION"

20 WAYS TO BLESS YOUR CHILDREN

1. Write a letter to your children on each of their birthdays, telling them why you value them. Present the collection of letters to them in a bound notebook on their thirtieth birthday.

2. Put together a "wall of fame" featuring pictures of key members of your children's heritage.

3. Do a study of your family tree, and present it to each child when he or she is old enough to appreciate it.

4. Visit a key historical landmark at least once a year, and tell how it played a vital part in their heritage.

5. Pray for the future of each member of your family every day.

6. Live below your means.

7. Get out of debt.

8. Create at least one dilemma per week for each child. Make it something that compels him or her to utilize principles that you've taught in order to get out of the dilemma.

9. Attend your child's parent/teacher meetings.

10. Pray for your child's teacher and principal every day.

11. Write out a list of each child's greatest strengths, and look for an opportunity to compliment her or him at least once a week.

12. Pray for the parents of your child's future spouse.

13. Intentionally cancel important plans in order to spend time with each child.

14. Kiss and hug your spouse in front of your children on a regular basis.

15. Buy at least one heirloom-quality gift for each of your children each year (a quality picture, pocketknife, fishing lure, etc.) that he or she can save as a childhood memory.

16. Make a "Very Special Person" plate, and feature each child twice a year.

17. Make sure that you, as parents, are the first to explain the facts of life to your child.

18. Keep a daily journal of the key things that your children say and do. It will be invaluable when they are older.

19. Have a planning weekend once a year when you and your spouse get away from the kids in order to spend time planning out the development of their character in the coming year.

20. Attend a Christian marriage seminar at least once a year.

TIM KIMMEL
CONDENSED FROM "LEGACY OF LOVE"

BUILDING YOUR CHILD'S FAITH

LET FAITH HAPPEN.
Your child will discover God in a whole host of ways—from the songs you sing to the way you comfort him when he cries. Everything you do for and with your child contributes to his understanding of love, which will eventually frame the way he understands God.

CREATE "GOD SIGHTINGS."
You can create "God sightings" by pointing out places where you see God's hand in your life. Thank God for your food, your clothes, your home, and show your child how to do the same. Notice God's creation whenever you can. Make God a real member of your family who is talked to and about often.

LOOK FOR GOD IN YOUR CHILD.
Pay attention to what God has placed in your child: an awareness of Christ, an affection for Him, a compassionate heart, a desire to pray, a sense of joy. Most of all, notice your child's curiosity about spiritual things.

STRENGTHEN YOUR OWN FAITH.
Let your child see you studying God's Word and prayerfully seeking His guidance.

ACCEPT THE MYSTERY.
Humbly accept that there will be parts of your child's faith that you don't understand, and trust that God is holding your child tenderly in His hand. Growing the faith of our children is perhaps our most sacred task as parents, but we are merely partners with our great God in this journey.

MARY MASLEN
EARLY CHILDHOOD DEVELOPMENT SPECIALIST

HOW TO RAISE TOTALLY AWESOME KIDS

❧ **Encouragement is the fuel for a healthy sense of self-worth.**
In order to build a child's sense of self-worth, a parent must look for every opportunity to recognize internal character qualities such as courage, honesty, fairness, compassion, perseverance, and kindness.

❧ **Demonstrate unconditional love.**
When your children receive unconditional love, they develop a deep sense of confidence, security, and reassurance, which their mistakes cannot erase.

❧ **Avoid comparisons.**
Comparing your kids with others will leave them feeling depressed and discouraged.

❧ **Separate the incident from the individual.**
There's a big difference between someone who *made a mistake* and someone who *is a mistake,* between someone who *told a lie* and someone who *is a liar.*

❧ **Recognize effort and celebrate progress.**
Principle-centered parents who want to build character and develop their child's sense of self-worth will focus on effort rather than on outcome, on progress rather than on performance.

❧ **Avoid reliving past failures.**
Focus on a child's strengths, without mentioning past failures.

DR. CHUCK AND JENNI BORSELLINO
CONDENSED FROM "HOW TO RAISE TOTALLY AWESOME KIDS"

WHEN PARENTS GET DISCOURAGED...

Keep the schedule simple.

Get plenty of rest.

Eat nutritious meals.

Stay on your knees.

DR. JAMES DOBSON
FROM "PARENTING ISN'T FOR COWARDS"

A PARENT'S COMMITMENT TO PRODIGAL CHILDREN

I will...

- Encourage.

- Keep communication open at all times.

- Permit person-to-person collect phone calls.

- Let them know they are loved and welcome at home, *always*.

- Permit the children to disagree with me, provided they do it respectfully. (And I find occasionally they are right and I am wrong.)

- Make a clear distinction between moral and nonmoral issues.

- Encourage.

RUTH BELL GRAHAM
FROM "PRODIGALS AND THOSE WHO LOVE THEM"

FAMILY

EIGHT STEPS TO GREAT COMMUNICATION

1. *Think before you speak.*
   Strive to accept your child as unconditionally as possible. Meet your child where he lives. He is much more likely to listen to what you have to say because you are not coming on strong or in a threatening way.

2. *Stress the positive.*
   Always look for encouraging ways to interact with your child. Emphasizing the positive side takes no longer than the negative, and the results are so much better.

3. *When you have to deal with the negative, do it in a positive, matter-of-fact way.*
   If your child comes home with something that doesn't belong to him, do not berate him or lecture him. Simply say in a matter-of-fact way, "That doesn't belong to you. Let's take it back to the owner." Then take him by the hand, walk him over to your neighbor's house, and have him return the item. Suggest to him that he say he is sorry he took it and that he won't do it again.

4. *Take time with your child.*
   Taking time with your child communicates that you really care. And I'm talking about special time—one-on-one—with each child each week. That's a tall order for most of us—but oh so worthwhile.

5. *Always be aware that you don't have to like what your child does, but you should always communicate that you love him and care about him.*

    When children misbehave, anger is a natural feeling. You do not have to be afraid to express your anger. But you must remember that your anger needs to be focused on the act or the behavior and not on the child.

6. *When you "blow it" with your children, ask their forgiveness.*

    This will accomplish two things. First, you will achieve much better communication with your children. Second, you will model how to ask forgiveness and help your children learn this difficult art.

7. *Keep in mind that results aren't always evident over the short term.*

    Parenthood is for the long haul. It is a long-range investment. If your child doesn't always respond to the techniques of reality discipline, don't give up.

8. *Ask for God's guidance daily, in your own life as well as in the lives of your children.*

    Let your prayer be that God's goodness will shine through your life in such a way that children will see the reality of your personal relationship with the almighty God.

DR. KEVIN LEMAN
ADAPTED FROM "MAKING CHILDREN MIND WITHOUT LOSING YOURS"

NURTURING COMPASSION

* NOTICE the needs and hurts of those around you.

* NEVER belittle, ridicule, or joke about someone's circumstances.

* IMAGINE with your children what it would be like to be handicapped.

* PRAY as a family for the difficulties of others.

* VISIT friends and relatives in the hospital.

* SHARE books and articles about people's challenges.

* TALK about how tragedies have impacted those you know.

* ASK your children how they'd feel if hard things happened to them.

* HELP the elderly in your neighborhood or church.

* TEACH your children not to be afraid of homeless people.

* BUY gifts for a needy family for Christmas.

* GO on a summer mission trip.

TAMI STEPHENS
MOTHER OF THREE

GIVE CHILDREN LOVE

Give the choice of love. Commit to love because it is right, not because it feels good.

Give the words of love. We all need regular verbal assurance; children need it the most.

Give the touch of love. Research has confirmed the human need for physical touch. The need to be held and cuddled is especially critical for babies.

Give the encouragement of love. Put courage into those little people by letting them know you are their best fan and cheerleader.

Give the comfort of love. In times of pain or sadness, provide love's healing comfort.

Give the laughter of love. Laughter sets a pleasant mood, a bright tone. Make merriment a daily dose of love in your home.

Give the discipline of love. Discipline establishes boundaries for children, making them feel safe and secure.

DONNA OTTO
FROM "FINDING A MENTOR, BEING A MENTOR"

FAMILY

CONNECTING WITH YOUR KIDS

TAKE A ONE-ON-ONE VACATION
Time alone with a parent during the teen years can be just the ticket for a teenager who needs to be reminded that she'll always have a safe haven as she moves out into the world.

PLAN A FAMILY NIGHT
Not only does Family Night give you an opportunity to spend some time together; it forces your kids to plan, budget, and take other people's likes and dislikes into consideration.

EAT DINNER TOGETHER
We make it a priority to sit down and eat a meal together at least five times a week. Not only is this a time to nourish your bodies with food; you nourish your family with good conversation and fun.

HAVE A DATE NIGHT
To create your own date night, ask your child what type of activity he'd enjoy. The object of your evening is to get out of the house and do something you will both enjoy and can talk about in the years to come.

PRAY TOGETHER
Pray for missionaries and math tests, friends who are sick, and puppies who are about to be born. No request is too trivial.

WRITE A LOVE NOTE

A family mailbox is a great way to encourage each other and brighten your kids' days. To start your own family mailbox, all you need is a basket, a pad of paper, and a pen. Start the ball rolling by writing notes to each member of your family.

BREAK FOR A TREAT

After a long day at school, kids need a chance to unwind before diving into their homework. Have popcorn and hot chocolate or cookies with a tall glass of frosty milk. This is when you find out about the day's happenings, how much homework there is, and, most important, how you can pray for your kids.

START A PARENT-CHILD JOURNAL

Find a notebook, attach a pen, then write a question to start the conversation. Ask about school, friends, books, or anything else that interests your child. Ask open-ended questions. This will help you get more in-depth responses, as well as having even more to write about the next time you share journal entries.

KATHI HUNTER
CHRISTIAN SPEAKER AND WRITER

AVOIDING THE SPENDING TRAP

BE A ROLE MODEL.

Kids are quick to pick up their parents' attitudes toward money. Track your own spending habits for a month; then determine how much of your money is going to wants as opposed to needs.

TALK ABOUT MONEY, A LOT.

Discuss finances with your kids. Talk to them about the dangers of credit card debt and the need to budget even small amounts of money. Don't be afraid to admit the mistakes you've made in your own life.

WATCH TV.

Sit with your kids for a half hour of after-school programming, and you'll be amazed at the number of advertisements targeted directly at them.

TURN OFF THE TV.

You can't isolate your kids completely from all the cool gadgets begging for their attention, but you can keep the sales pitches out of your home, and this is one way to do it.

SHOP WITH YOUR KIDS.

Use your weekly trip to the grocery store as an object lesson. Before you go, have the kids clip coupons and help write the grocery list. Once you're at the store, talk to them about the purchases you make.

TAKE ADVANTAGE OF SPECIAL OCCASIONS.

If your son has been begging for the latest game or designer jeans, have him add it to his birthday or Christmas list. This way, he appreciates the item more and learns a lesson in patience as well.

GIVE THEM A JOB.

Even small jobs—setting the table, mowing the lawn, or keeping their rooms clean—give kids a sense of pride, self-discipline, and a work ethic.

SET LIMITS.

If your daughter needs a new pair of jeans, decide on an amount that you feel is reasonable for the purchase. If your daughter wants a more expensive pair, require her to earn the difference.

TEACH THEM TO TITHE THEIR MONEY...

Encourage your children to give 10 percent of their earnings. That doesn't necessarily mean it has to go in the offering plate. Help them sponsor a child or purchase toys to be sent to needy children at Christmas.

...AND THEIR TIME.

Get the whole family involved in community outreach. Deliver food baskets, clean up litter in your neighborhood, or spend some time at a local nursing home or homeless shelter.

LISA JACKSON
ADAPTED FROM "CHRISTIAN PARENTING TODAY" MAGAZINE

HOW TO STOP FAMILY BICKERING

EXAMINE YOURSELF FIRST

If we want our children to treat each other with kindness and patience, we have to model those traits constantly. Kids are especially tuned in to the words we say and how we say them.

HEAD 'EM OFF AT THE PASS

If you really want to reduce the bickering, start looking for what triggers problems between your children. If there are predictable causes for conflict, work to eliminate those causes before the problems start.

SPEAK WORDS OF LIFE

The Word has plenty to say about the destructive nature of the tongue. You can also use Ephesians 4:29 to deal with bickering. It states, "Do not let any unwholesome talk come out of your mouths, but only what is helpful for building others up according to their needs, that it may benefit those who listen." In this way you can turn battles into opportunities for spiritual growth.

FOCUS ON THE FRUITS

Bickering isn't just an annoyance; it's a sign of the selfish nature each of us battles as we work to be more like Jesus. By taming these behaviors in our children, we are doing much more than simply preserving peace in the here and now. We are training our children to walk in the Spirit for a lifetime.

～

KEEP YOUR PERSPECTIVE—AND A SENSE OF HUMOR

As never ending as these years can seem, remember that childish squabbles and teenage fights won't last forever. Keep in mind your goal of developing godly character in your children, and be thankful for the small victories along the way.

～

PRAY, PRAY, PRAY!

We are imperfect parents raising imperfect children in a fallen world. However, God's grace is sufficient to get your family through even the most difficult times. Being on our knees on behalf of our children is the greatest gift we can give them.

THERESA B. LODE
FREELANCE WRITER

10 WAYS TO TEACH YOUR CHILDREN INTEGRITY

1. Drive the speed limit.

2. Never ask your child to lie for you.

3. Apologize when you wrong your children.

4. Send them into a store with more money than they need to buy a particular item. When they come out, see if they offer the change.

5. Never tolerate even the smallest lie.

6. Pick someone out of the newspaper who committed a crime, and ask the kids' opinion about it.

7. Fathers, never allow your sons to be disrespectful or rude to their mother.

8. Set up tasks that require their follow-through without supervision, and see if they carry out instructions on their own.

9. Take your children to visit their ancestors' graves. If you know any anecdotes about these ancestors, take time to share a few stories.

10. Have them memorize twenty verses on integrity. (You might want to start with the Ten Commandments.)

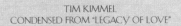

TIM KIMMEL
CONDENSED FROM "LEGACY OF LOVE"

10 WAYS TO TEACH YOUR CHILD DISCIPLINE

1. Take your children to juvenile court to listen to some cases. Afterward take them out for a soda and discuss the subject of "consequences."

2. Have them study a musical instrument long enough to learn about the discipline of practice.

3. Enroll them in a team sport where their faithful attendance and participation is required.

4. Assign daily chores and hold them responsible to perform them.

5. Have them tithe every Sunday from their allowance.

6. Make sure that they complete homework.

7. Have them write to a missionary once a month.

8. Give them an alarm clock, show them how to use it, and have them assume the responsibility of getting up on time for school for a whole year!

9. Help them memorize an elaborate poem.

10. Take them to a junkyard and show them the wreckage of cars involved in alcohol-related accidents.

TIM KIMMEL
CONDENSED FROM "LEGACY OF LOVE"

HELPING YOUR KIDS SUCCEED

* *Set clear standards.* Be certain your child knows what is expected of him or her.

* *Expect the best.* Communicate that you believe in your child and that he or she can do what is expected.

* *Pay attention.* Catch your child doing things well.

* *Personalize recognition.* Let your son or daughter know specifically what you appreciate and why.

* *Tell the story.* Don't be afraid to brag about what your child does right.

* *Celebrate together.* As a family, intentionally celebrate when one member accomplishes something significant.

* *Set the example.* It's essential that you, as the parent, practice what you preach.

JAMES. M. KOUZES AND BARRY Z. POSNER
ADAPTED FROM "ENCOURAGING THE HEART"

FAMILY RULES

- Be kind and forgive others.
  EPHESIANS 4:32
- Treat your body as a temple of God.
  1 CORINTHIANS 6:19-20
- Husbands, love your wives sacrificially.
  EPHESIANS 5:25, 33
- Wives, submit to your husbands as to the Lord and respect them.
  EPHESIANS 5:22, 33
- Give to God's work.
  2 CORINTHIANS 9:6-8
- Children, honor and obey your parents.
  EPHESIANS 6:1-3
- Do not provoke your children, but carefully teach them about God.
  EPHESIANS 6:4
- Do not be bound together with unbelievers.
  2 CORINTHIANS 6:14
- Respect those in authority.
  ROMANS 13:1
- Do not lie to one another.
  COLOSSIANS 3:9
- Do not use coarse, filthy language.
  EPHESIANS 5:4
- Do your work the best you can.
  COLOSSIANS 3:23

DR. RICK FOWLER AND JERILYN FOWLER
PRESTONWOOD COUNSELING CENTER

BENEFITS OF LESS TELEVISION

CHILDREN LEARN TO ENTERTAIN THEMSELVES.

When we provide basic tools, our children turn out some amazing creations. Towers emerge from blocks and castles arise from the sandbox.

❧

CHILDREN LEARN CRUCIAL THINKING SKILLS WHILE ENTERTAINING THEMSELVES.

As educational as many children's television shows are, they are not truly interactive. Games that actively involve a child stimulate cognitive abilities and develop crucial thinking skills.

❧

PLAY ENCOURAGES PROBLEM SOLVING AND CAN LENGTHEN A CHILD'S ATTENTION SPAN.

When children play, they are forced to think about how things interact and fit together. They learn to figure things out—all by themselves. Concentrating on finding these solutions also helps children focus, which can develop their attention span.

IT KEEPS KIDS MOVING.

Watching an inordinate amount of television can be a risk factor for childhood obesity. Children who watch an excessive amount of TV tend to be more sedentary, less likely to engage in sporting activities, have poor eating habits, and have a higher incidence of obesity.

❧

YOUR VALUES BECOME THEIR VALUES.

As children grow and watch more network and cable TV, they are exposed to an overwhelming array of messages that do not reflect biblical standards. Even "safe" programs often send a clear message that wealth, beauty, and power are fundamental to happiness. Instead of allowing the television to usurp our authority, we can reclaim control.

❧

YOU'LL HAVE MORE FAMILY TIME.

When the TV is on, the family is tuned in but not to one another. If we want our kids to value family time, we have to demonstrate that it's a priority.

KIRSETIN KARAMARKOVICH MORELLO
FREELANCE WRITER AND MOTHER OF TWO BOYS

ADVICE TO PARENTS

Treasure the good times.

Let go of the bad times.

Forgive your children.

Forgive yourself.

Never get off your knees.

ANNETTE SMITH
ADAPTED FROM "HELP! MY LITTLE GIRL'S GROWING UP"

8
Community

Building healthy relationships

THE WALK OF LOVE

THE WALK OF LOVE
releases others from your expectations.
You unconditionally set yourself up to exhibit
Christ's love regardless of their actions.

THE WALK OF LOVE
is expressed in a servant spirit.
You look to channel your talents and energies
toward encouraging and stimulating others.

THE WALK OF LOVE
is sacrificial.
You are willing to give up your time
and even your ambition
for the sake of seeking first the kingdom of God.

CHARLES STANLEY
FROM "A GIFT OF LOVE"

LOVE IS...

SLOW TO SUSPECT...*quick to trust.*

SLOW TO CONDEMN...*quick to justify.*

SLOW TO OFFEND...*quick to defend.*

SLOW TO REPRIMAND...*quick to forbear.*

SLOW TO BELITTLE...*quick to appreciate.*

SLOW TO DEMAND...*quick to give.*

SLOW TO PROVOKE...*quick to conciliate.*

SLOW TO HINDER...*quick to help.*

SLOW TO RESENT...*quick to forgive.*

BARBARA JOHNSON
FROM "FRESH ELASTIC FOR STRETCHED OUT MOMS"

BE AN ENCOURAGER

~ ENCOURAGEMENT
   is a gift.

~ ENCOURAGEMENT
   creates energy.

~ ENCOURAGEMENT
   lasts a lifetime and can be life-changing.

~ ENCOURAGEMENT
   motivates positive behavior.

~ ENCOURAGEMENT
   is often the most effective form of motivation.

~ ENCOURAGEMENT
   more often comes from listening than talking.

~ ENCOURAGEMENT
   is more effective than criticism.

~ ENCOURAGEMENT
   can be as simple as a smile.

~ ENCOURAGE
   everyone you know and everyone you meet.

BRUCE AND STAN
ADAPTED FROM "GOD IS IN THE SMALL STUFF"

GIVE AND TAKE

→ *The more you give,*
the more you get.

→ *The more you love,*
the less you fret.

→ *The more you do unselfishly,*
the more you live abundantly.

→ *The more of everything you share,*
the more you'll always have to spare.

→ *The more you love,*
the more you'll find that
life is good and friends are kind.

→ *For only what we give away*
enriches us from day to day.

DAVID AND CLAUDIA ARP
FROM "MARRIAGE PARTNERSHIP" MAGAZINE

SHARING 101

➤PRINCIPLE 1

Everything you have comes from God.

➤PRINCIPLE 2

Everything that is given to you is given in trust to you.

➤PRINCIPLE 3

The blessings that you have are not just for your own personal benefit.

➤PRINCIPLE 4

What is given to you is given that you might share it with others.

RAY PRITCHARD
FROM "AND WHEN YOU PRAY"

FIVE REASONS WE NEED FRIENDS

1.

FRIENDS PROVIDE PERSPECTIVE

No matter how capable you are, there will be days you feel lost, when you need some clear direction, some fresh ideas, or just a different perspective. That's what friends are for.

2.

FRIENDS PROVIDE COMPANY

Good friends provide a distraction from the pressures of your day, comfort from the hurts of life, and escape from loneliness. Sometimes friends laugh with you and sometimes they cry with you, but most important, friends are always willing to be with you when you need them.

3.

FRIENDS PROVIDE A PLACE TO VENT

Some days you can handle the difficulties that press you down; other days you just have to let it all out. A friend is willing to listen when you just feel like complaining about the injustices and annoyances that fill this world.

4.

FRIENDS PROVIDE ACCOUNTABILITY

To be accountable is to consent to being watched and questioned. Allowing yourself to be transparent and vulnerable is a wonderful protection against temptation and naïveté. You let them catch you when you fall and lift you back to the place where you know you should be.

5.

FRIENDS PROVIDE ENCOURAGEMENT

Sometimes it's easy to lose hope. The frustrations of the past haunt you, the stress of the present overwhelms you, and the prospect of the future discourages you. When you are overwhelmed, you need at least one cheerleader.

DR. STEVE STEPHENS AND ALICE GRAY
CONDENSED FROM "THE WORN OUT WOMAN"

RELATIONSHIPS WILL STRUGGLE IF...

- ✒ You are accountable to no one.

- ✒ Your opinion is always more important than the opinion of others.

- ✒ You are quarrelsome.

- ✒ You find it difficult to be a team player.

- ✒ You are always right about everything.

- ✒ You find it difficult to say "I'm sorry" without defending yourself or blaming others.

- ✒ You refuse to take help.

- ✒ You are unteachable.

- ✒ You are unable to recognize others' accomplishments or rejoice in their successes.

- ✒ You are unable to say, "I'm hurting; I'm in trouble."

- ✒ You never reverse your path when wrong, but make only minor adjustments.

- ✒ You always think, *This message is for someone else, not me.*

MICHAEL L. BROWN
CONDENSED FROM "REVOLUTION IN THE CHURCH"

YOU CAUSE OTHERS
TO STUMBLE WHEN...

→ You allow negativity to grow.

→ You compromise your integrity.

→ You break your promises.

→ You speak before thinking.

→ You act out of greed or selfishness.

→ You refuse to forgive.

→ You twist the truth.

→ You justify your behavior.

→ You hurt others.

→ You leave God out of your decisions.

DR. STEVE STEPHENS
AUTHOR AND SEMINAR SPEAKER

COMMUNITY

ANGER HURTS OTHERS WHEN...

You hold onto it too long.

You refuse to forgive.

You attack the person, not the action.

You let it become a habit.

You lose control.

You become abusive.

You hurt those you love.

You react rather than act.

You dwell on it constantly.

You damage someone's reputation.

JOHN VAN DIEST
ASSOCIATE PUBLISHER

WHAT CARING FRIENDS WILL DO

† Set aside quality time for you.

† Pray for you.

† Help you out when needed.

† Show you respect.

† Stand up for you.

† Listen to you without distraction.

† Keep your secrets.

† Give godly counsel.

† Laugh with you.

† Cry with you.

† Believe the best in you.

† Forgive graciously.

† Reflect God's love to you.

ALICE GRAY
AUTHOR AND SEMINAR SPEAKER

WHAT CARING FOR OTHERS MEANS

*Many might have failed beneath the bitterness of their
trial had they not found a friend.*
CHARLES HADDON SPURGEON

⁓

*Treat people as if they were what they ought to be and you help
them to become what they are capable of being.*
JOHANN WOLFGANG VON GOETHE

⁓

*A real friend is one who walks in when the
rest of the world walks out.*
WALTER WINCHELL

⁓

*Our love for God is best proved by our regard
for the needs of our neighbors.*
BILLY GRAHAM

⁓

*Friends are those rare people who ask how we
are and then wait to hear the answer.*
ED CUNNINGHAM

Great opportunities to help others seldom come,
but small ones surround us every day.
SALLY KOCH

Never hesitate to hold out your hand;
never hesitate to accept the outstretched hand of another.
POPE JOHN XXIII

When you say a situation or a person is hopeless,
you are slamming the door in the face of God.
CHARLES L. ALLEN

Life's most persistent question is:
What are you doing for others?
MARTIN LUTHER KING JR.

Friends are divinely placed guardrails.
STU WEBER

EIGHT REASONS TO GO TO CHURCH

1. Church worship celebrates God's presence.

2. Worship gives you an opportunity to talk with God.

3. Worship makes spiritual things real.

4. Regular church attendance will keep you out of harmful places.

5. Church attendance keeps you focused on eternity.

6. Volunteering to help out at church makes your life fruitful.

7. Worshipping with other believers brings heaven to earth.

8. Church attendance keeps you accountable.

JAMES A. SCUDDER
CONDENSED FROM "YOUR SECRET TO SPIRITUAL SUCCESS"

TIPS FOR FINDING A GOOD CHURCH

A good church clearly proclaims the whole counsel of God as revealed in the Old and New Testaments of the Bible. A good church is a teaching church.

✝

A good church has a system of accountability within which people are held responsible for their lifestyle and disciplined when they unrepentingly rebel against God's standards.

✝

A good church has a comprehensive view of ministry. It applies the Scripture to every area of life and therefore has (or is seeking to develop) ministries that impact every member of the family.

✝

A good church has a passion to win people to Christ and see them develop in the faith, and therefore it emphasizes evangelism and discipleship.

✝

A good church supports the weak, helps the needy, and encourages the downhearted. It prioritizes ministry to those who are less fortunate.

TONY EVANS
FROM "THE VICTORIOUS CHRISTIAN LIFE"

LIFESTYLE EVANGELISM

BE ENTHUSIASTIC

Are you enthusiastic about your faith in Jesus Christ? Contagious Christians are doing something that's got them excited, something that gets them out of bed in the morning.

BE AUTHENTIC

People don't only read the Christian literature we give them; they read our lives. It's nearly impossible to ignore someone who authentically lives out his or her convictions. But it's easy to discount someone who says one thing and does another.

LOOK FOR OPPORTUNITIES

In the past month, how many of you have had dinner with an unsaved couple or individual? Witnessing presents a real challenge if we are always around believers.

BE PREPARED

Prepare yourself for evangelism by praying and studying the Bible. Begin on your knees by asking God to touch your unsaved friends through the power of the Holy Spirit. Even if you don't see your friends come to Christ right away, keep praying!

START TODAY

Nothing can compare to being God's instrument to lead one person out of the kingdom of Satan into the glorious life of heaven. If you have never had that experience, or you would like to be more effective in your witness, God can use you starting today.

DR. DAVID JEREMIAH
ADAPTED FROM "TURNING POINTS"

BECOMING "FISHERS OF MEN"

† Go when you feel like it and when you don't.

† Go by faith and not by feeling.

† Go when it's convenient and when it's not.

† Go in season and out of season.

† Go when you have fished all night and caught nothing.

† Go when you succeed and when you fail.

FLOYD MCELVEEN
FROM "UNASHAMED"

SHARING THE GOSPEL

❧ *Pray* before going.

❧ *Ask* for and claim the filling of the Holy Spirit.

❧ *Commit* to Him all your fears and inadequacies.

❧ *Learn to live* by faith, not by feelings.

❧ *Learn to love* by faith.

❧ *Confess* all known sin and forsake it.

❧ *Claim* God's wisdom, love, compassion, and boldness.

❧ *Carry* your New Testament with you always.

❧ *Expect* God to use you.

❧ *Show* key verses as well as quoting them.

Be courteous. Never argue; listen well.

Show them their hopelessness apart from Jesus Christ.

Show clearly the need for repentance toward God.

Demonstrate clearly from Scripture that Jesus is the only way.

Anticipate objections; answer them before they come up.

Stress the necessity of being certain of salvation.

Stress the urgency of salvation.

Speak of the joy of abundant life in Christ.

Cast a vision of the wonder and sweet solace of heaven.

FLOYD MCELVEEN
CONDENSED FROM "UNASHAMED"

9

Success

Making the most of life

BREAKING OUT OF THE RUT

ASSUME
responsibility for your own life.
Refuse to be either an excuser (rationalize failure)
or an accuser (blame others).
Instead be a chooser, and choose to break out of the rut you're in.

BELIEVE
you can change!
Stop saying "I can't" and start saying "I can."

CLARIFY
what you really want.
Write down specifically how you'd like to change.

DON'T WAIT
for ideal circumstances.
Stop saying "When things settle down…" Do it now!
"One of these days" is really none of these days.

RICK WARREN
AUTHOR OF "THE PURPOSE-DRIVEN LIFE"

　SUCCESS

EIGHT BENEFITS OF A
POSITIVE ATTITUDE

1.
Increased enthusiasm

2.
Freedom from the limitations of fear

3.
Increased creativity

4.
Enjoyment in taking the initiative

5.
Exciting joy when using more of your God-given potential

6.
Boundless opportunities

7.
Abundance of positive friends and colleagues

8.
Increased efficiency in utilizing your time and energy

PAUL J. MEYER
FROM "UNLOCKING YOUR LEGACY"

EIGHT IMPORTANT GOALS

1.
To walk in the Spirit daily

2.
To serve God in the fullness of the Holy Spirit's
guidance and power

3.
To maximize my full potential

4.
To use all of my talents and abilities in the way
God created them to be used

5.
To fulfill God's purpose for my life

6.
To experience and enjoy life to its fullest

7.
To have a feeling of deep and abiding satisfaction that
I have fulfilled God's goals for my life

8.
To know the joy that comes in knowing Christ

CHARLES STANLEY
FROM "SUCCESS GOD'S WAY"

TESTS FOR DECISION MAKING

✔ SCRIPTURAL TEST

HAS GOD ALREADY SPOKEN ABOUT IT IN HIS WORD?

All Scripture is God-breathed and is useful for teaching, rebuking, correcting and training in righteousness. (2 Timothy 3:16)

✔ SECRECY TEST

WOULD IT BOTHER ME IF EVERYONE KNEW THIS WAS MY CHOICE?

The integrity of the upright guides them, but the unfaithful are destroyed by their duplicity. (Proverbs 11:3)

✔ SURVEY TEST

WHAT IF EVERYONE FOLLOWED MY EXAMPLE?

Set an example for the believers in speech, in life, in love, in faith and in purity. (1 Timothy 4:12)

✔ SPIRITUAL TEST

AM I BEING PEOPLE-PRESSURED OR SPIRIT-LED?

Am I now trying to win the approval of men, or of God?... If I were still trying to please men, I would not be a servant of Christ. (Galatians 1:10)

✔ STUMBLING TEST
COULD THIS CAUSE ANOTHER PERSON TO STUMBLE?
It is better not to eat meat or drink wine or to do anything else that will cause your brother to fall. (Romans 14:21)

✔ SERENITY TEST
HAVE I PRAYED AND RECEIVED PEACE ABOUT THIS DECISION?
Do not become anxious about anything, but in everything, by prayer and petition, with thanksgiving, present your requests to God. And the peace of God, which transcends all understanding, will guard your hearts and your minds in Christ Jesus. (Philippians 4:6–7)

✔ SANCTIFICATION TEST
WILL THIS KEEP ME FROM GROWING IN THE CHARACTER OF CHRIST?
And we, who with unveiled faces all reflect the Lord's glory, are being transformed into his likeness. (2 Corinthians 3:18)

✔ SUPREME TEST
DOES THIS GLORIFY GOD?
So whether you eat or drink or whatever you do, do it all for the glory of God. (1 Corinthians 10:31)

JUNE HUNT
FROM "HOPE FOR THE HEART"

21 PRINCIPLES FOR
SPIRITUAL LEADERS

1. No experience, good or bad, is ever wasted.

2. People may apply for various leadership positions, but God is the one who ultimately determines which leadership roles they will have.

3. God's assignments are always based on character—the greater the character, the greater the assignment.

4. The role of spiritual leaders is not to dream up dreams for God, but to be the vanguard for their people in understanding God's revelation.

5. The real key to God's promises is not people or physical resources, but God.

6. The definitive measure of leaders' success is whether they moved their people from where they were to where God wanted them to be.

7. In God's eyes, *how* something is done is as important as *what* is done. The end does not justify the means in God's kingdom.

8. God has a specific agenda for every person and every organization.

9. The single most important thing leaders should do is pray.

10. The reason there are not more great spiritual leaders in our day is that there are not more men and women willing to pay the price.

11. Effective leaders are sensitive to the nuances of their words.

12. A pessimistic leader is a contradiction in terms.

13. Leaders should pay close attention to their attitudes, for these serve as barometers to the condition of their hearts.

14. Spiritual leaders are not discouraged by their circumstances—they are informed by them.

15. Spiritual leaders make every decision with the awareness that one day they will give an account to God.

16. Once leaders clearly understand God's will, deciding how to invest their time becomes much easier.

17. God does not give people more than they can handle, but people regularly assume responsibility for things they should not be doing.

18. The quantity of work leaders can accomplish is in direct proportion to their ability to delegate work to others.

19. Spiritual leaders cannot rush in and out of God's presence.

20. Leaders don't jump to conclusions. They process the facts and seek to determine the truth of their situation.

21. Spiritual leaders are not haphazard people. They are intentional.

HENRY AND RICHARD BLACKABY
CONDENSED FROM "SPIRITUAL LEADERSHIP"

THE ROLE OF SPIRITUAL LEADERS

THE SPIRITUAL LEADER'S TASK IS TO MOVE PEOPLE FROM
WHERE THEY ARE TO WHERE GOD WANTS THEM TO BE.
Once spiritual leaders understand God's will, they make every
effort to move their followers from following their own agenda to
pursuing God's purposes.

SPIRITUAL LEADERS DEPEND ON THE HOLY SPIRIT.
They seek to move people on to God's agenda, all the while being
aware that only the Holy Spirit can ultimately accomplish the task.

SPIRITUAL LEADERS ARE ACCOUNTABLE TO GOD.
They assume their responsibility is to move people to do God's will.
Until they do this, they have not yet fulfilled their role as leaders.

SPIRITUAL LEADERS CAN INFLUENCE ALL PEOPLE,
NOT JUST GOD'S PEOPLE.
History is replete with examples of Christian men and women
exerting spiritual leadership upon secular society.

SPIRITUAL LEADERS WORK FROM GOD'S AGENDA.
God's concern is not to advance leaders' dreams and goals or to
build their kingdoms. His purpose is to turn His people away
from their self-centeredness and their sinful desires and to draw
them into a relationship with Himself.

HENRY AND RICHARD BLACKABY
CONDENSED FROM "SPIRITUAL LEADERSHIP"

20 QUALITIES OF GODLY LEADERS

1. Respected.
2. Faithful to marriage.
3. Even-tempered.
4. Self-disciplined.
5. Friendly and accessible.
6. Knowledgeable about what they talk about.
7. Not given to drunkenness.
8. Not pushy or overbearing.
9. Not petty or quarrelsome.
10. Not driven by money or things.
11. A good manager of their home.
12. Attentive to their spouse and children.
13. Honest and humble.
14. Wise.
15. Fair with others.
16. Committed to what is good.
17. Devoted to what is right.
18. Empowered by what is true.
19. Strong and steadfast in their faith.
20. Able to encourage and correct.

THE APOSTLE PAUL
ADAPTED FROM 1 TIMOTHY 3:2–7 AND TITUS 1:6–9

WHEN GOD GIVES THE DREAM

+ A GOD-GIVEN DREAM
  will stir your passion.

+ A GOD-GIVEN DREAM
  will be humanly impossible to accomplish.

+ A GOD-GIVEN DREAM
  will make an impression on you for a lifetime.

+ A GOD-GIVEN DREAM
  will cause you to exercise strong faith.

+ A GOD-GIVEN DREAM
  will be attacked by the enemy of our souls.

INJOY STEWARDSHIP SERVICES
FROM "40 DAYS OF FASTING AND PRAYER"

FOUR SECRETS OF LIFE

❧

Establish specific goals for your life.

❧

Persevere when you encounter failure.

❧

Build financial security.

❧

Listen to your critics.

ROBERT JEFFRESS
CONDENSED FROM "THE SOLOMON SECRETS"

HOW TO BREAK A BAD HABIT

1.
ASK WHY.
Why do I want to change?
Why is this habit interfering with life?

2.
WRITE OUT YOUR ANSWERS.
Be honest and concrete in your description.
Listing consequences gives motivation for change.

3.
CONFIDE IN A FRIEND.
Confession is good for the soul.
Accountability helps you succeed.

4.
BE PURPOSEFUL.
Establish a plan.
Good intentions alone accomplish nothing.

5.
TAKE THE FIRST STEP.
Beginning is often the hardest part.
Don't expect God to do what you can do yourself.

6.
PERSEVERE.
Remember, habits feel comfortable.
New habits "scratch" and take time to embrace.

7.
AVOID TEMPTATION.
Flee when the old habit tempts.
Go a different direction; call a friend.

8.
THINK, DON'T FEEL.
Feelings change moment by moment.
Make wise choices based on knowledge.

9.
READ SCRIPTURE.
Saturate yourself in the Psalms.
They contain promises for strength.

10.
RELY ON GOD'S HELP.
Remember, God is there to help you.
"Call to me and I will…tell you great and unsearchable things."
(JEREMIAH 33:3)

GLENDA HOTTON
PROFESSOR OF HOME ECONOMICS, MASTER'S COLLEGE

BE A WINNER

The winner is always part of the answer.
The loser is always part of the problem.

The winner always has a program.
The loser always has an excuse.

The winner says, "Let me do it for you."
The loser says, "That is not my job."

The winner sees an answer for every problem.
The loser sees a problem for every answer.

The winner sees a green near every sand trap.
The loser sees a sand trap near every green.

The winner says it may be difficult but it is possible.
The loser says it may be possible but it is too difficult.

BARBARA JOHNSON
FROM "FRESH ELASTIC FOR STRETCHED OUT MOMS"

PRINCIPLES OF POSITIVE CRITICISM

✔ NEVER POINT OUT ERRORS WITHOUT OFFERING A SOLUTION.
The time for correction must also become a time to
teach.

✔ CRITICIZE THE ACT, NEVER THE PERSON.
Why deflate someone's ego when your goal is to
improve performance? People have emotions that
need to be respected.

✔ NEVER SCOLD IN PUBLIC.
Even if the error is minor, don't embarrass
someone by pointing out mistakes in front of
colleagues.

✔ ALWAYS END WITH PRAISE.
Some people believe you should start with a
compliment and end with correction. I reverse it—
preferring to end on a positive note.

NEIL ESKELIN
CONDENSED FROM "LEADING WITH LOVE"

SUCCESS

CULTIVATE THE MIND OF CHRIST BY BECOMING...

APPRECIATIVE

I thank my God every time I remember you.

PHILIPPIANS 1:3

CONSIDERATE

If what I eat causes my brother to fall into sin,
I will never eat meat again,
so that I will not cause him to fall.

1 CORINTHIANS 8:13

HUMBLE

I am less than the least of all God's people.

EPHESIANS 3:8

SERVANTLIKE

A servant of Christ Jesus.

ROMANS 1:1

CONFIDENT

I can do everything through him who gives me strength.

PHILIPPIANS 4:13

EXCITED

I am convinced that neither death nor life...nor any-
thing else in all creation, will be able to separate us
from the love of God that is in Christ Jesus our Lord.

ROMANS 8:38–39

A GOAL-SETTER
I plan to…go to Spain.
ROMANS 15:24

PERSISTENT
For two whole years Paul stayed there….
Boldly and without hindrance he preached the kingdom
of God and taught about the Lord Jesus Christ.
ACTS 28:30-31

A POSITIVE THINKER
If God is for us, who can be against us?
ROMANS 8:31

VICTORIOUS
The Lord will rescue me from every evil attack and will
bring me safely to his heavenly kingdom.
2 TIMOTHY 4:18

DALE GALLOWAY
FROM "ON-PURPOSE LEADERSHIP"

ATTITUDE IS EVERYTHING

YOUR BASIC ATTITUDE AFFECTS YOUR BELIEF
IN YOUR POTENTIAL FOR SUCCESS.

A negative attitude causes you to doubt your ability to achieve, while belief in your potential makes you willing to take the necessary action for success.

YOUR ATTITUDE DETERMINES WHAT
YOU THINK ABOUT FACING A CHALLENGE.

People with a negative attitude see a challenge as overwhelming or threatening. A positive attitude lets you see a challenge as an opportunity rather than a threat.

YOUR ATTITUDE DETERMINES YOUR CONFIDENCE.

People with negative attitudes have so often thought *I can't* or *I doubt* that belief in their individual potential is nonexistent. Each time you act from a positive attitude, your self-confidence is enhanced, your ability to achieve is proven, and you know you can succeed.

YOUR ATTITUDE AFFECTS HOW YOU SEE OPPORTUNITY.

People who have a negative attitude have buried the ability to see opportunity. A positive attitude, by contrast, opens your eyes to so many opportunities that your challenge becomes which opportunity to choose.

PAUL J. MEYER
ADAPTED FROM "UNLOCKING YOUR LEGACY"

YOU MAY BE A "CONTROL-AHOLIC"

If you...

+ never do anything spontaneous.

+ fall apart when your schedule is interrupted.

+ have to look just right every time you go out.

+ yell at your children excessively about messing up the house.

+ have to have everything matching.

+ spend an inordinate amount of time planning, organizing, and seeking to emulate that seemingly perfect friend.

+ need to know exactly what to expect of a given event or circumstance.

+ can't relax until "all the work is done."

+ feel uncomfortable with mystery, randomness, unanswered questions.

ELIZABETH CODY NEWENHUYSE
CONDENSED FROM "SOMETIMES I FEEL LIKE RUNNING AWAY FROM HOME"

SUCCESS

40 BEHAVIORS TO AVOID

1. Obsessing over regrets
2. Saying "yes" to the wrong things
3. Saying "no" to the right things
4. Buying into materialism
5. Seeking fulfillment from others
6. Setting foolish priorities
7. Setting no priorities
8. Speaking without considering the consequences
9. Avoiding long-term commitments
10. Becoming negative or critical
11. Not anticipating the future
12. Clinging to the past
13. Submitting to fear
14. Being paralyzed by worries
15. Refusing to get help
16. Ignoring problems while they're small
17. Making false assumptions
18. Limiting oneself
19. Limiting God
20. Not learning from mistakes

21. Avoiding responsibility
22. Blaming others
23. Enjoying a rut
24. Majoring on minors
25. Minoring on majors
26. Hurting others
27. Becoming cynical
28. Thinking above the law
29. Thinking inside the box
30. Not pacing oneself
31. Using people
32. Speaking more than listening
33. Placing comfort above character
34. Believing only what you see
35. Seeing only what you believe
36. Overreacting to situations
37. Denying blind spots and weaknesses
38. Fighting change
39. Not affirming people
40. Losing perspective

ALICE GRAY, STEVE STEPHENS, JOHN VAN DIEST
EDITORS

KEY PEOPLE FOR A MINISTRY TEAM

A VISIONARY
Someone who sees everything the ministry could be in ten years. This person could also be a bit of a dreamer who has fresh ideas for ministry.

A SHEPHERD
A leader with a heart for people. Someone who cares about what is being taught, who is teaching, and what the results are.

AN ADMINISTRATOR
A leader who gets things done. Usually has good follow-through and pays attention to details.

AN ENCOURAGER

A cheerleader. One who is enthusiastic and reminds people that our strength is in the Lord.

A WORKER

Similar to the administrator in his or her get-it-done giftedness. This person is not always interested in being in charge but is willing to work until a task is completed. A great planner and doer.

A PRAYER WARRIOR

You will know this person when you meet him or her. It is someone who will be the foundation of your team. One who will always be in prayer for the ministry and will encourage others to pray over everything.

ROBYNE BEAUBIEN
EDITOR, WOMEN'S MINISTRY CENTRAL CONSULTING

HARD WORK

Beats talent almost every time

Almost always leads to success

Helps eliminate regrets

Increases the likelihood of
personal satisfaction and happiness

PAT WILLIAMS
FROM "SECRETS FROM THE MOUNTAIN"

10
Wisdom

Learning from the experience of others

THREE STAGES IN EVERY
GREAT WORK OF GOD

✝

IT IS IMPOSSIBLE.

✝

IT IS DIFFICULT.

✝

IT IS DONE.

~

J. HUDSON TAYLOR
MISSIONARY TO CHINA

WHAT IS LIFE?

Life is a gift…ACCEPT IT.

Life is an adventure…DARE IT.

Life is a mystery…UNFOLD IT.

Life is a game…PLAY IT.

Life is a struggle…FACE IT.

Life is beauty…PRAISE IT.

Life is a puzzle…SOLVE IT.

Life is opportunity…TAKE IT.

Life is sorrowful…EXPERIENCE IT.

Life is a song…SING IT.

Life is a goal…ACHIEVE IT.

Life is a mission…FULFILL IT.

DAVID MCNALLY
FROM "EVEN EAGLES NEED A PUSH"

NEVER...

Lose one moment of time,
to improve it in the most profitable way I can.

Do anything I should despise or think
meanly of in another.

Do anything out of revenge.

Do anything that I should be afraid to do if it
were the last hour of my life.

JONATHAN EDWARDS
THEOLOGIAN AND PHILOSOPHER

THE WISDOM OF JESUS

Jesus...

- modeled love and sacrifice.

- was always faithful to His word and vision.

- embraced His purpose.

- lived so He had nothing to hide.

- shared His heart with God.

- counted the cost.

- refused to give up.

- faced temptation head-on.

- asked great questions.

- knew where to go for help.

- believed the best in people.

- listened beyond a person's words.

- maintained a positive attitude.

- did not allow popularity to dictate decisions.

- looked at life with eternity in mind.

- prayed before every decision.

- placed people before schedules.

- balanced truth and love.

- chose His words carefully.

- gave grace to all who would accept it.

- finished well.

BILL PERKINS
PRESIDENT OF MILLION MIGHTY MEN

LOVE IS A GREAT THING

† It lightens every burden.

† It passes smoothly over all misfortunes.

† It turns bitterness into something sweet.

† It spurs us on to great things.

† It soars to the heights.

† It knows no limits.

† It aims beyond its strength.

† It refuses to admit impossibility.

THOMAS Á KEMPIS
ADAPTED FROM "THE IMITATION OF CHRIST"

APPRECIATE SIMPLICITY

* Simplicity adds quality and contentment to your life.

* Simplicity comes from learning to say "no."

* Simplicity is being as satisfied with what you don't have as with what you have.

* Simplicity involves removing the clutter.

* Simplicity means never buying something for the purpose of impressing others.

* Simplicity refuses to get caught in the trap of overspending, overcommitting, and overworking.

* Simplicity enjoys happiness and treasures joy.

* Simplicity cherishes tranquillity.

* Simplicity knows how to be content in whatever situation you find yourself.

* Simplicity celebrates God's creation and sees God in the small stuff.

BRUCE AND STAN
ADAPTED FROM "GOD IS IN THE SMALL STUFF"

10 GEMS OF WISDOM

1.
No thought can contain Him,
no word can express Him;
He is beyond anything we can intellectualize or imagine.

2.
Living out of the false self creates a compulsive desire
to present a perfect image to the public so that
everybody will admire us and nobody will know us.

3.
Silent solitude forges true speech.

4.
It is God who has called us by name;
the God beside whose beauty the Grand Canyon
is only a shadow has called us beloved.

5.
In every encounter we either give life or we drain it.
There is no neutral exchange.

6.

Hope knows that if great trials are avoided,
great deeds remain undone and the possibility of
growth into greatness of soul is aborted.

7.

Genuine faith leads to knowing the love of God,
to confessing Jesus as Lord,
and to being transformed by what we know.

8.

The truth of faith has little value when
it is not also the life of the heart.

9.

The promised peace that the world cannot give
is located in being in right relationship with God.

10.

If we search for one word to describe the mission and ministry of
Jesus Christ, *reconciliation* would not be a bad choice.

BRENNAN MANNING
FROM "THE RABBI'S HEARTBEAT"

CORE TRUTHS

⚜ In God's economy, nothing that happens to you is ever wasted.

⚜ Planning, organization, and maintenance can help make your hard times easier.

⚜ Relationships—with God and with others—are the most important treasures you can stock up in your life.

⚜ Time is short. Don't put off doing what you know to do.

⚜ God can use even your negative experiences for His good purposes.

⚜ Don't worry! When you open your hands in need—even if you've neglected to prepare—God will not let you down.

EMILIE BARNES
FROM "A DIFFERENT KIND OF MIRACLE"

THE WORDS OF A SAINT

† Find time to pray without ceasing.

† Every wound is not healed with the same remedy.

† The times demand you to guide others to safe havens.

† The crown is immortality.

† Stand strong like a beaten anvil.

† It is the part of a good athlete to be bruised and to prevail.

† Consider the times: Look for Him who is above time.

† Slight not those who serve you.

† Let your stewardship define your work.

† A Christian is not his own person, but waits upon God.

ST. IGNATIUS
CHURCH FATHER OF CONSTANTINOPLE

SEVEN DEADLY SINS

SLOTH
The sin by which we ignore our obligations

LUST
The sin that never delivers what it promises

ANGER
The sin that wants revenge for wrongs done against us

PRIDE
The sin that mars so many ministries

ENVY
The sin that keeps us from caring
for the grass on our side of the fence

GLUTTONY
The sin that abuses what God has made

GREED
The sin that enjoys abundance at the expense of others

TONY CAMPOLO
FROM "SEVEN DEADLY SINS"

10 LIES ABOUT SIN

1. Sin is no big deal.

2. A little sin won't hurt.

3. Taking radical action against sin isn't necessary.

4. God won't mind a little compromise.

5. It's my body; I can do what I want with it.

6. I can control my drives.

7. I won't experience any consequences for my sin.

8. God is keeping something good from me.

9. The pleasure sin promises is better and more real than God's pleasure.

10. Fulfilling my sin will satisfy me.

JOSHUA HARRIS
ADAPTED FROM "NOT EVEN A HINT"

WORDS ON WISDOM

It is comforting to know that not only the steps
but also the stops of a good man are ordered by the Lord.
GEORGE MUELLER

Judge each day not by its harvest, but by the seeds you plant.
AUTHOR UNKNOWN

It is the fire of suffering that brings forth the gold of godliness.
MADAME GUYON

Relying on God has to begin all over again every day.
C. S. LEWIS

Time is a very precious gift of God;
so precious that it's only given to us moment by moment.
AMELIA BARR

Never mistake knowledge for wisdom.
One helps you make a living; the other helps you make a life.
SANDRA CAREY

⁓

The secret of patience…is to do something else in the meantime.
AUTHOR UNKNOWN

⁓

All men desire peace, but very few desire
those things that make for peace.
THOMAS À KEMPIS

⁓

The most important things in life aren't things.
CHURCH BULLETIN

⁓

You were made by God and for God—
until you understand that, life will never make sense.
RICK WARREN

⁓

THE QUALITIES OF WISE PEOPLE

They...

→ bring joy to their father (Proverbs 10:1).

→ work hard (Proverbs 10:5).

→ accept instruction (Proverbs 10:8).

→ treasure knowledge (Proverbs 10:14).

→ listen to others (Proverbs 12:15).

→ stay calm when insulted (Proverbs 12:16).

→ think before they act (Proverbs 13:16).

→ walk with those who are wise (Proverbs 13:20).

→ look ahead to see what is coming (Proverbs 14:8).

→ act cautiously and avoid danger (Proverbs 14:16).

→ make learning a joy (Proverbs 15:2).

→ are hungry for truth (Proverbs 15:14).

→ use few words (Proverbs 17:27).

→ manage their anger (Proverbs 29:11).

KING SOLOMON
FROM THE HOLY BIBLE

SEVEN TIMES NOT TO SPEAK

1.

Don't speak too much.

PROVERBS 10:19

2.

Don't speak when angry.

PROVERBS 12:16

3.

Don't speak harshly.

PROVERBS 14:15

4.

Don't speak before thinking.

PROVERBS 15:28

5.

Don't speak boastfully.

PROVERBS 17:19

6.

Don't speak until you hear both sides.

PROVERBS 18:17

7.

Don't speak of things said in confidence.

PROVERBS 20:19

KING SOLOMON
FROM THE HOLY BIBLE

WISDOM

PLANS FOR TODAY

- To awake each morning with a smile brightening my face;

- To greet the day with reverence for the opportunities it contains;

- To approach my work with a clean mind;

- To hold ever before me, even in the doing of the little things, the ultimate purpose toward which I am working;

- To meet men and women with laughter on my lips and love in my heart;

- To be gentle and kind and courteous through all the hours;

- To approach the night with weariness that ever woos sleep and the joy that comes from work well done—

This is how I desire to waste wisely my days.

THOMAS DEKKER
PLAYWRIGHT

ALWAYS REMEMBER THIS

WHEN GOD SPEAKS,
listen.

WHEN GOD COMMANDS,
obey.

WHEN GOD LEADS,
follow.

BRUCE AND STAN
FROM "GOD IS IN THE SMALL STUFF"

11
Virtue

Strengthening your character

WHY SETTLE FOR...

...*bitterness* when you could have *love*?

...*detachment* when you could *connect* with other people?

...*pettiness* when you could grow in *maturity*?

...*self-absorption* when you could *help others*?

...*compulsive performance* when you could have *grace*?

...*scorekeeping* when you could have *mercy*?

...*the way it used to be* when *today* has so much potential?

...*the way it ought to be* when you could create a better reality?

...*burdensome grudges* when you could experience the freedom of forgiveness?

...*pride* when you could walk in *godly humility*?

...*power* and *self-will* when you could learn the true power of *submission*?

...*denial* when you could have *honesty* and *awareness*?

...*less* than the *best* that God has for you?

~~~

STEPHEN ARTERBURN
FROM "FLASHPOINTS"

HOW TO SAFEGUARD
YOUR CHARACTER

- Take regular time for reflection and restoration of your soul.

- When faced with an ethical choice or temptation, consider the example you set for others.

- Make yourself accountable to a small group of trusted friends.

- Focus on integrity, not image.

- Grow deep in your faith.

- Deal firmly and uncompromisingly with hidden sin and character flaws.

- Make a commitment to pursue lifelong character growth.

PAT WILLIAMS
FROM "THE PARADOX OF POWER"

FIVE QUALITIES THAT CHANGE YOUR HEART

1) *Conviction*—the recognition that worldly and selfish motives have robbed our homes and our souls of our spiritual destiny.

2) *Repentance*—the determination to change direction and to pursue the life of the kingdom.

3) *Humility*—the willingness to seek out new paradigms and new patterns for life priorities.

4) *Perseverance*—the commitment to press toward freedom in the face of disappointments and failures.

5) *Passion*—the desire for intimacy with God that fuels our pursuit of His presence as the central focus of our lives.

JEROME DAILEY
ADAPTED FROM "SOUL SPACE"

VIRTUE

HOW TO LIVE A HOLY LIFE

EMBRACE THE CALL TO HOLINESS.
Personal purity and dedication to Christ are not
optional for a believer.

> *For God did not call us to be impure,*
> *but to live a holy life.*
>
> 1 THESSALONIANS 4:7

DEVELOP A CHRISTLIKE CHARACTER.
Recognize that holiness is not just avoiding public
sin. Holiness is as much about what you do as what
you don't do.

> *But just as he who called you is holy,*
> *so be holy in all you do.*
>
> 1 PETER 1:15

ALLOW GOD TO TRANSFORM YOU THROUGH HIS WORD.
Scripture reveals the mind of Christ and God's purposes and direction for our lives.

> *Do not conform any longer to the pattern of this world,*
> *but be transformed by the renewing of your mind.*
> *Then you will be able to test and approve what God's will is—*
> *his good, pleasing and perfect will.*
>
> ROMANS 12:2

NURTURE A RECEPTIVE HEART.

We can only grow in holiness if we are willing to listen and yield to the Holy Spirit.

So, as the Holy Spirit says:
"Today, if you hear his voice, do not harden your hearts
as you did in the rebellion."

HEBREWS 3:7-8

CHOOSE YOUR FRIENDS CAREFULLY.

Those we spend time with will influence us.

Do not be misled:
"Bad company corrupts good character."

1 CORINTHIANS 15:33

BE PATIENT.

Holiness is a process and not an appointment. Godly character is born of the "little" daily decisions to deny selfishness and follow Christ.

Then he said to them all:
"If anyone would come after me, he must deny himself
and take up his cross daily and follow me."

LUKE 9:23

DR. CHAD GARRISON
CALVARY BAPTIST CHURCH

PRIDE VS. TEACHABILITY

➤ PRIDE FILTERS OUT.
> The teachable listen in.

➤ PRIDE NARROWS ITS GAZE.
> The teachable welcome surprise.

➤ PRIDE KNOWS ALL THE ANSWERS.
> The teachable ask questions.

➤ PRIDE NURTURES BLIND SPOTS.
> The teachable go to where the light is.

➤ PRIDE MEMORIZES THE LETTER OF THE LAW.
> The teachable get the Spirit.

STEVEN MOSLEY
FROM "SECRETS OF THE MUSTARD SEED"

THE VALUE OF INTEGRITY

---

† Integrity serves as a guide in life's moral decisions.
PROVERBS 11:3

† Integrity hates falsehood in every form.
PROVERBS 13:5-6

† Integrity is something to be held onto, even in tough times.
JOB 2:3

† Integrity keeps its word even when it hurts.
PSALM 15:1-4

† Integrity isn't afraid to run when evil comes knocking.
2 TIMOTHY 2:22

† Integrity says both *yes* and *no* and means what it says.
JAMES 5:12

† Integrity backs up what it says with how it lives.
TITUS 2:7

† Integrity is what God looks for in a person's character.
1 CHRONICLES 29:17

TERRY BROWN AND MICHAEL ROSS
FROM "COMMUNICATE"

PROTECTING YOUR INTEGRITY

1.
REMAIN ON GUARD AT ALL TIMES.
Remember that temptation rarely comes to us as an obvious assault, but usually as a sly subterfuge, a deceptive ploy.

2.
BE ESPECIALLY CAREFUL ABOUT TEMPTATION
WHEN YOU ARE AT AN EMOTIONAL OR PHYSICAL LOW POINT.
You know that when you are feeling discouraged, needy, lonely, abandoned, and dejected, it is easy to reach for something to fill that emptiness or relieve that pain.

3.
SET CLEAR BOUNDARIES AND LIMITS
FOR YOURSELF AHEAD OF TIME.
You cannot make good moral and ethical decisions under the pressure of temptation. You must make a deliberate decision about the way you will live your life before temptation comes, and then it will be easier for you to stick to a decision you have already made.

4.
FILL YOUR LIFE WITH GOOD THINGS AND GOOD PEOPLE
SO THERE IS LESS ROOM FOR TEMPTATION.
We are more prone to temptation when we are feeling empty and unfulfilled. So the answer is to fill our lives with good things, meaningful activities, and healthy relationships with positive people so that temptation won't be able to gain a toehold in our lives.

5.
WHEN TEMPTED, PRAY.

Ask God for help in maintaining your integrity. When you feel you lack the strength within yourself to resist temptation, rely on God's strength.

6.
RECITE SCRIPTURE.

If you study and memorize the Scriptures, you will be armed in advance against the enemy of your integrity.

7.
WHEN YOU FAIL, LEARN AND GROW FROM YOUR FAILURE.

Learn from your moral failure, stop sinning and straying, put your failures behind you, and walk in a new direction.

PAT WILLIAMS
FROM "HOW TO BE LIKE JESUS"

IF YOU BYPASS VIRTUE

- ⊰ It won't make you happy in the long haul.

- ⊰ It hurts you.

- ⊰ It forces you to lie to yourself and others.

- ⊰ It models bad behavior.

- ⊰ It demonstrates immaturity.

- ⊰ It blocks personal growth.

- ⊰ It undermines your character.

- ⊰ It damages your reputation.

- ⊰ It plants future problems.

- ⊰ It makes it easier to repeat a mistake.

- ⊰ It sabotages your mental health.

- ⊰ It hardens your heart.

- ⊰ It callouses your conscience.

- It builds a wall between you and God.

- It corrodes spiritual insight and perspective.

- It creates health difficulties.

- It twists and confuses your thinking.

- It disappoints those you love.

- It establishes negative patterns for your children.

- It plays into Satan's hands and promotes his ways.

- It smears God's reputation.

- It discourages other Christians.

- It slows God's work in the world.

- It saddens God.

- It leads to death.

DR. STEVE STEPHENS
AUTHOR AND SEMINAR SPEAKER

AVOID THESE COMMON SINS

Absorbed with self. Adultery. Anger. Bad debts. Bitterness. Broken friendship. Carelessness. Cheating. Covetousness. Demandingness. Disloyalty. Divisiveness. Envy. Gossip. Greed. Homosexual behavior. Impatience. Independence. Jealousy. Lack of commitment to church. Laziness. Losing one's temper. Lying. Lust. Moral indifference. Neglect of the Lord's Supper. Petty complaining. Pornography. Prayerlessness. Pride. Property damage. Recurring sin. Resentment. Self-righteousness. Sexual impurity. Strained family relationship. Substance abuse. Thanklessness. Theft. Tithing neglected. Unbelief. Worry.

LUIS PALAU
FROM "SAY YES! HOW TO RENEW YOUR SPIRITUAL PASSION"

SCRIPTURES THAT COMMUNICATE VIRTUE

⊸ The value of hard work: Proverbs 6:6–9 and 14:23

⊸ The value of correction: Proverbs 12:1

⊸ The value of listening: Proverbs 1:8–9 and 4:1

⊸ The value of humility: Proverbs 18:12

⊸ The value of obedience: Ephesians 6:1–2

⊸ The value of doing good: Romans 12:18–21

⊸ The value of contentment: 1 Timothy 6:6

⊸ The value of overlooking an offense: Matthew 5:39–45

⊸ The value of bringing peace: Matthew 5:9

⊸ The value of hospitality: Hebrews 13:2

⊸ The value of controlling anger: James 1:20

SCOTT TURANSKY AND JOANNE MILLER
CONDENSED FROM "GOOD AND ANGRY"

WHAT PREVENTS SIN IN
THE CHRISTIAN LIFE

Reading the Bible
"I have hidden your word in my heart,
that I might not sin against you."
PSALM 119:11

❦

The Prayers of Jesus
"I'm not asking you to take them out of the world,
but to keep them safe from the evil one."
JOHN 17:15

❦

Being Controlled by the Holy Spirit
"Those who are dominated by the sinful nature
think about sinful things, but those who are
controlled by the Holy Spirit think about
things that please the Spirit."
ROMANS 8:5

Letting God Transform
"Don't copy the behavior and customs of this world,
but let God transform you into a new person
by changing the way you think."

ROMANS 12:2

❧

Being on Guard
"Watch out for attacks from the Devil,
your great enemy.... Take a firm stand against him,
and be strong in your faith."

1 PETER 5:8–9

❧

Wearing All Spiritual Armor
"Put on all of God's armor so that you will be
able to stand firm against all strategies
and tricks of the Devil."

EPHESIANS 6:11

SCRIPTURES FROM THE NEW LIVING TRANSLATION

POWER PRINCIPLES FOR CHRISTIAN SERVICE

❒ The foundation of ministry is character.

❒ The nature of ministry is service.

❒ The motive for ministry is love.

❒ The measure of ministry is sacrifice.

❒ The authority of ministry is submission.

❒ The purpose of ministry is the glory of God.

❒ The tools of ministry are the Word of God and prayer.

❒ The privilege of ministry is growth.

❒ The power of ministry is the Holy Spirit.

❒ The model for ministry is Jesus Christ.

DAVID WIERSBE AND WARREN W. WIERSBE
FROM "MAKING SENSE OF THE MINISTRY"

WHAT FAITHFULNESS MEANS

→ *Faithfulness Means Excellence*
Faithfulness doesn't necessarily mean doing *more,* but doing things *better.* Doing our best in every situation is one proof of faithfulness.

→ *Faithfulness Means Integrity*
Faithfulness means that we are above moral reproach at all times. Remember: God still sees us, even when no one is watching.

→ *Faithfulness Means Dependability*
Faithful people can be relied upon to fulfill their commitments. When a job is delegated to a faithful worker, the boss never has to worry if the job will get done.

→ *Faithfulness Means Perseverance*
Lots of people start running the race of life with a flash, but few finish well. Others might get side-tracked or drop out of the race, but we must keep running with our eyes fixed on Jesus. Faithfulness means that we persevere to the finish line.

KENT CROCKETT
CONDENSED FROM "MAKING TODAY COUNT FOR ETERNITY"

TURNING FOES INTO FRIENDS

Find ways to compliment your enemies.
> *Bless those who persecute you; bless and do not curse.* (Romans 12:14)

Repay evil with good toward your enemies.
> *Do not repay anyone evil for evil. Be careful to do what is right in the eyes of everybody.* (Romans 12:17)

Intercede in prayer for your enemies.
> *But I tell you: Love your enemies and pray for those who persecute you.* (Matthew 5:44)

Empathize with your enemies.
> *Rejoice with those who rejoice; mourn with those who mourn.* (Romans 12:15)

Nurture a forgiving heart toward your enemies.
> *Do not take revenge, my friends, but leave room for God's wrath, for it is written: "It is Mine to avenge; I will repay," says the Lord. Do not be overcome by evil, but overcome evil with good.* (Romans 12:19, 21)

Decide to love your enemies.
> *Let no debt remain outstanding, except the continuing debt to love one another, for he who loves his fellowman has fulfilled the law.* (Romans 13:8)

Seek to fulfill the needs of your enemies.
> *If your enemy is hungry, feed him; if he is thirsty, give him something to drink. In doing this, you will heap burning coals on his head.* (Romans 12:20)

JUNE HUNT
FROM "HOPE FOR THE HEART"

WHAT FORGIVENESS DOES

 Forgiveness embraces the offender.
By forgiving—and welcoming back—those who
hurt Him the most, Christ modeled forgiveness at
its best.

 Forgiveness is proactive.
When Jesus was on the cross, He said, "Father,
forgive them; for they do not know what they are
doing" (Luke 23:34). To be like Jesus, we must also
forgive people before they even ask for it.

 Forgiveness surrenders the right to get even.
The essence of forgiveness is letting go of my rights
to punish and see justice done. Forgiveness is
evident when one ceases to demand restitution for
hurt feelings and wounded pride.

DENNIS AND BARBARA RAINEY
CONDENSED FROM "TWO HEARTS PRAYING AS ONE"

SEVEN STEPS OF FORGIVENESS

STEP #1:

FACE THE HURT.

This may sound strange, but the first step toward forgiving another person is actually to admit how hurt and angry you really are.

STEP #2:

TALK IT OUT.

Explain your perspective and feelings as calmly as you can, and invite the other person to do the same—then listen. Seeing the other person's side may not reduce the pain, but it can soften your heart and help you forgive.

STEP #3:

REMEMBER WHY FORGIVENESS MATTERS.

Jesus wants you to forgive others—not necessarily because they deserve it, not even because forgiving is good for you (though it is), but because He forgave you first.

STEP #4:

CHOOSE FORGIVENESS.

This means you make a decision of the will, deliberately giving up your right to make others pay for the hurts they have caused.

STEP #5:

PUT THE HURT BEHIND YOU.

Forgetting isn't necessary—and may not be possible—but you need to stop rehearsing the pain over and over again. When memories arise (they will), choose to put them away and focus on other things.

STEP #6:

BE PATIENT WITH THE PROCESS.

Forgiveness is rarely a simple, one-time proposition. If you've been deeply hurt, you might have to go through the whole process more than once. With God's help, you'll get there—and your reward will be peace and freedom.

STEP #7:

FORGIVE YOURSELF.

It's hard to forgive others if you can't forgive yourself. Even when you feel that the guilt-producing secrets you carry in your heart are too horrible for forgiveness, extend to yourself the same grace you are trying to extend to others—the same grace God has already extended to you.

ALICE GRAY
FROM "THE WALK OUT WOMAN"

VIRTUE

RANDOM ACTS OF RIGHTEOUSNESS

† Witnessing to someone about Jesus
1 CORINTHIANS 9:16–17

† Seeking God diligently
HEBREWS 11:6

† Giving money for God's work
MATTHEW 6:3–4, 19–20

† Praying
MATTHEW 6:6

† Fasting
MATTHEW 6:17–18

† Budgeting money wisely
LUKE 16:11–12

† Serving the Lord faithfully in ministry
LUKE 19:17; 1 CORINTHIANS 15:58

† Helping others
LUKE 6:35

† Loving those who don't love in return
MATTHEW 5:46

† Treating others with honor
MATTHEW 10:41

† Being a godly spouse and parent
1 PETER 3:3–7

✝ Working faithfully in earthly jobs
COLOSSIANS 3:22–24

✝ Doing good deeds
EPHESIANS 6:7–8

✝ Submitting with respect to unreasonable employers
1 PETER 2:18–20

✝ Being persecuted for His name's sake
LUKE 6:22–23

✝ Having a servant's attitude
MARK 10:43–45

✝ Humbling ourselves
MATTHEW 18:4

✝ Doing little things for others
MATTHEW 10:42

✝ Helping the poor
PROVERBS 19:17

✝ Visiting widows and orphans in their distress
JAMES 1:27

✝ Living righteously
PROVERBS 11:31

KENT CROCKETT
CONDENSED FROM "MAKING TODAY COUNT FOR ETERNITY"

12
Comfort for the Tough Times

FOUR THINGS THAT
MAKE TRIALS EASIER

1.
It helps
when I know who is in control.

2.
It helps
when I know I'm not alone in my suffering.

3.
It helps
when I know the purpose of God behind it.

4.
It helps
because I become more compassionate with
and understanding of others.

RUTH BELL GRAHAM
FROM "PRODIGALS AND THOSE WHO LOVE THEM"

NOTHING CAN SEPARATE US
FROM GOD'S LOVE

---

† Not death

† Not life

† Not angels

† Not demons

† Not fears for today

† Not worries for tomorrow

† Not the greatest powers

† Not the highest star

† Not the deepest ocean

† Not anything in all creation

ST. PAUL THE APOSTLE
ROMANS 8:38–39

THE COMFORTER

The Holy Spirit is our...

COUNSELOR
One Who relieves another of mental distress.

HELPER
One Who furnishes with relief or support.
One Who is of use and who waits upon another.

INTERCESSOR
One Who acts between parties to reconcile differences.

ADVOCATE
One Who pleads the cause of another.

STRENGTHENER
One Who causes another to grow,
become stronger, endure, and resist attacks.

STANDBY
One Who can be relied upon
either for regular use or in emergencies.

ANNE GRAHAM LOTZ
FROM "JUST GIVE ME JESUS"

GOD CAN!

The Lord our God is worthy.

He can do anything but fail.

He can comfort lonely hearts.

He can change adverse circumstances.

He can heal diseased bodies.

He can mend broken relationships.

He can move our mountains.

He can conquer our worst enemies.

He can fix every problem.

He can guide every footstep.

He can heal our deepest hurts.

He can forgive our worst sins.

He can lift our heaviest burden.

He can calm our worst storms.

He can satisfy our deepest hunger.

Bless His holy name.

REV. DR. GEOFFREY V. GUNS
SELECTED FROM "THE PURPOSE OF WORSHIP"

THE GOOD SHEPHERD

❧ HE OWNS THE SHEEP:
      they belong to Him.

❧ HE GUARDS THE SHEEP:
      He never abandons them when danger is near.

❧ HE KNOWS THE SHEEP,
      knows them each by name and leads them out.

❧ HE LAYS DOWN HIS LIFE FOR THE SHEEP,
      such is the measure of His love.

BILLY GRAHAM
FROM "TILL ARMAGEDDON"

WHERE TO LOOK

Look up.
God will never leave or forsake you.
His Word is a light unto your path.

Look out.
Confide in a friend.
Seek comfort and counsel in local resources.

Look in.
Take an inventory of your feelings.
Journal your thoughts, ideas, and progress.

Look for truth.
Gather information and research your options.
Often natural inclinations are in opposition to God's ways.

Look realistically.
Resist the temptation to change others.
Change what you can; accept what you cannot.

Look for balance.
Take care of yourself.
Get enough rest; eat healthfully; attempt to simplify life.

Look for laughter.
A cheerful heart is like good medicine.
Choose joyful music, uplifting books, optimistic friends.

Look for hope.
This too shall pass.
Dwell on what is good and worthy of praise.

Look for comfort.
Read the Psalms.
Let others encourage you and find ways to encourage others.

Look for God's purpose.
Every experience has spiritual significance.
Press closer to God and allow Him to deepen your faith.

GLENDA HOTTON
PROFESSOR OF HOME ECONOMICS, MASTER'S COLLEGE

WHEN GOING THROUGH DIFFICULTIES

Remember...

❦

God knows what I am going through.

❦

God uses my trials to help me grow.

❦

God calls me to rejoice in my pain.

❦

God invites me to submit to my faithful Creator.

RAY PRITCHARD
FROM "THE GOD YOU CAN TRUST"

I WILL TRUST...

The power of God to guide me,

The might of God to uphold me,

The wisdom of God to teach me,

The eye of God to watch over me,

The ear of God to hear me,

The Word of God to speak to me,

The hand of God to protect me,

The way of God to lie before me,

The shield of God to shelter me,

The hosts of God to defend me.

Christ with me, Christ before me,

Christ beneath me, Christ above me,

Christ at my right, Christ at my left,

Christ in breadth, Christ in length,

Christ in height, Christ in the heart...

ST. PATRICK
THE PATRON SAINT OF IRELAND

HEALING YOUR EMOTIONAL WOUNDS

Open yourself to God for cleaning out the wound.

╬

Practice forgiveness.

╬

Pray for anyone who despitefully uses you.

╬

Give others the benefit of the doubt,
even those who hurt you.

╬

Let God heal your broken spirit.

╬

Overcome evil by doing good.

DALE GALLOWAY
FROM "ON-PURPOSE LEADERSHIP"

GOD'S STRESS MANAGEMENT PLAN

≈ WORK OUT your difficulties with others.

≈ HELP those around you.

≈ REJOICE in the Lord always.

≈ SLOW DOWN and be gentle.

≈ REMEMBER that "God is near."

≈ LET GO of all your anxieties.

≈ HAND them over to God.

≈ ALLOW God's peace to guard your heart and mind.

≈ FOCUS on the positives of life.

≈ DO what you already know you should do.

≈ BE CONTENT with whatever situation you are in.

≈ CLAIM the promise that "I can do everything through Him who gives me strength."

≈ ACCEPT the help and encouragement of others.

≈ TRUST God to meet all your needs.

≈ GIVE God all the glory.

THE APOSTLE PAUL
LETTER TO THE PHILIPPIANS, CHAPTER 4

FIVE THINGS NOT TO WORRY ABOUT

1.
YOUR TREASURES HERE ON EARTH—
money, investments, possessions

2.
YOUR EVERYDAY LIFE—
the basics of food and water

3.
YOUR BODY—
health, safety, death

4.
YOUR APPEARANCE—
what you wear

5.
YOUR FUTURE—
all that tomorrow might bring

JESUS
MATTHEW 6:19–34

HOW TO R-E-S-T FROM WORRY

Renew your mind constantly with God's Word; look for God's attributes/character; study and dig deeply to know God intimately.

Express total dependence on the Lord for the day, acknowledging and confessing sin, weaknesses, and struggles.

Satisfy your heart in Christ alone! Pray Psalm 90.

Take all that comes into your life as from the Lord and trust Him! Your times are in His hand.

BRENDA WHEALY
FROM "THE BEST THING I EVER DID FOR MY MARRIAGE"

12 WAYS TO OVERCOME DISCOURAGEMENT

1. TAKE CARE OF THE PHYSICAL.
Eat right. Get plenty of rest. Exercise regularly. Go for walks. Keep the lights on (especially during bleak winter months).

2. KNOW YOURSELF.
What does recovery time look like to you? Know if it means time alone, time with others, time for exercise, time for sleep. Plan some recovery time right away, without retreating.

3. REACH OUT FOR THE HELP OF OTHERS.
Ask for it, whether practical help with housework, church responsibilities, or whatever. And ask for encouragement.

4. KEEP AN ENCOURAGEMENT FILE.
When someone writes you a nice note, save it! And don't forget to send encouraging notes to others.

5. LISTEN TO UPLIFTING CHRISTIAN MUSIC.
Both the Old and New Testaments talk a lot about the importance of worship music.

6. LIMIT YOUR INVOLVEMENT.
Don't spend a lot of time with discouraging, critical people. Also avoid discouraging movies, books, or music.

7. PRAY CONTINUALLY.
You may not feel close to God, but discouragement should always drive us to the Lord.

8. LEARN A SPIRITUAL DISCIPLINE.

Choose a Scripture verse to memorize and review. Or find someone you can pray for. Spiritual disciplines lift us closer to the Lord—and out of discouragement.

9. LOOK BACK TO SEE WHAT GOD HAS DONE IN THE PAST.

Consider the bigger picture. Then consider the Artist of the bigger picture. Don't try to usurp His role. As someone once said, "For peace of mind, please resign as master of the universe."

10. WRITE DOWN YOUR EXPECTATIONS.

What do you expect for yourself, your children, your spouse, your church, your home, your friendships, the holidays, etc.? Then consider: Are these expectations realistic? Which are under my control? What will I do to meet these expectations? Which are highest in priority?

11. ANTICIPATE AREAS OF RECURRING DISCOURAGEMENT.

Have a plan for specific trouble areas and times that you know will be hard emotionally.

12. CONTINUE TO OBEY!

The reason God gives us such an open window in the Scriptures into the lives of His people is so that we can learn—and gain courage for our own lives. So walk by the Spirit, and the Lord will lift your spirits.

RENÉE S. SANFORD
BIBLE TEACHER AND SEMINAR SPEAKER

SHOWING GOD'S LOVE

† TO SPEAK a healing word to a broken heart.

† TO EXTEND a hand to one who has fallen.

† TO GIVE a smile to those whose laughter has been lost.

† TO ENCOURAGE the dreamer who has given up.

† TO SHARE the painful solitude of one who is alone.

† TO EASE the burden of one bent low beneath a thankless task.

† TO REASSURE the doubter and reinforce the believer.

† TO LIGHT the candle of God's Word in the midst of another's darkest night.

BARBARA JOHNSON
FROM "HE'S GONNA TOOT AND I'M GONNA SCOOT"

WHEN OUR CHILDREN DISAPPOINT US

FACE THE TRUTH.

Fear often stops when we have the courage to confront it. If we suspect that our children are involved in something unhealthy, we need to ask them about it. It takes courage to hear difficult truths from those we love, but it is better than not knowing.

BE WILLING TO LISTEN WHEN THEY WANT TO TALK.

The hardest thing for children to do is admit that they have disappointed us. It is difficult for them to say, "I was wrong."

PRAYER IS ESSENTIAL.

When hard things hit, sometimes all we can do is trust, be thankful that God is there, and pray. He knows our children, and He can work effectively in their lives. As you pray, anticipate the blessing.

RECOGNIZE THAT THERE IS A POINT OF RELEASE.

With older children, a time may come when we need to free ourselves from them for a while. Otherwise, they can break our hearts daily.

RELINQUISH OVER AND OVER AND OVER.

Sometimes the road to restoration must be paved with relinquishment and forgiveness. Christian families are not immune to crisis, but those who arm themselves with knowledge, prayer, and love have a better rate of survival.

BARBARA BAUMGARDNER
ADAPTED FROM "DECISION" MAGAZINE

SEVEN LESSONS FROM JOB

One
In this life man will never know all of God's wisdom and in some respects is not even in a position to ask the question, "Why?"

⁓

Two
Although it is not always readily noticeable, the wicked will one day come to judgment.

⁓

Three
The notion that suffering is always the result of sin is totally destroyed.

⁓

Four
Man is in no position to justify his own situation by accusing God of injustice.

Five
Theological niceties are not likely to
stop the tears of one who is suffering.

Six
God's people are challenged to recognize with humility the
sovereignty of God and to trust that in His wisdom there
truly is a time and purpose for all things.

Seven
Whether or not it is apparent, God is working in the
life of each individual to bring His people
into a closer relationship with Him.

DR. F. LAGARD SMITH, BIBLE SCHOLAR AND PROFESSOR
FROM "THE DAILY BIBLE IN CHRONOLOGICAL ORDER"

LORD OF MY HEART

Lord of my heart...

Give me vision to inspire me, that, working or resting,

I may always think of You.

Give me light to guide me, that, at home or abroad,

I may always walk in Your way.

Give me wisdom to direct me, that, thinking or acting,

I may always discern right from wrong.

Give me courage that, amongst friends or enemies,

I may always proclaim Your justice.

Give me trust to console me, that, hungry or well-fed,

I may always rely on Your mercy.

ANCIENT BRITISH PRAYER

13
Eternal Hope

Discovering "all is well"

GOD IS THERE

When the sky is dark—
He is there.

When you are all alone—
He is there.

When nothing goes your way—
He is there.

When you are in pain—
He is there.

When people are against you—
He is there.

When you are frightened or worried—
He is there.

When those you love are in crisis—
He is there.

When you feel as if God is far away—
He is there.

When doubt and confusion weigh you down—
He is there.

When you are about to breathe your last—
He is there.

And where God is, *there is always hope.*

DR. STEVE STEPHENS
AUTHOR AND SEMINAR SPEAKER

SIX EVENTS IN YOUR FOREVER LIFE

1. LIFE.
   You are created in the image of God for a life of purpose.

2. DEATH.
   You die physically, but not spiritually.

3. DESTINATION.
   You reach your destination after death, which is determined by what you believed on earth.

4. RESURRECTION.
   You receive a resurrected body.

5. REPAYMENT.
   You receive your reward or your retribution for eternity based on what you did on earth.

6. ETERNITY.
   You will live forever in the presence or absence of God, reaping the consequences of your beliefs and actions on earth.

BRUCE WILKINSON
FROM "A LIFE GOD REWARDS"

ETERNAL EYESIGHT

→ *Look* at life's storm as opportunities for eternal praise.

→ *Focus* your thoughts on the unseen spiritual world.

→ *See* your present circumstances as only temporary.

→ *Understand* that God is preparing a new body for you.

→ *Regard* inner strength as your new clothing.

→ *Recognize* that this life will always have loss and grief.

→ *Know* that aging is part of God's plan for your life.

→ *Depend* upon God's gift of the Holy Spirit in you as your source of strength.

→ *View* life through the eyes of faith.

→ *Look* forward to your eternal home with the Lord.

→ *Make* it your goal to please God.

→ *Remember,* you will appear before the judgment seat of Christ.

JUNE HUNT
FROM "HOPE FOR THE HEART"
BASED ON 2 CORINTHIANS 4:17–5:1

HOW HOPE ACTS

HOPE looks for the good in people instead of harping on the worst in them.

HOPE opens doors where despair closes them.

HOPE discovers what can be done instead of grumbling about what cannot be done.

HOPE draws its power from a deep trust in God and the basic goodness of mankind.

HOPE "lights a candle" instead of "cursing the darkness."

HOPE regards problems, small or large, as opportunities.

HOPE cherishes no illusions, nor does it yield to cynicism.

FOUNDER OF THE CHRISTOPHERS
FATHER JAMES KELLER, MM

WHAT WE CAN COUNT ON

GOD'S MERCY
for our past mistakes.

GOD'S LOVE
for our present needs.

GOD'S SOVEREIGNTY
for our future.

ST. AUGUSTINE
THEOLOGIAN AND PHILOSPHER

GOD'S ANSWERS

You say: It's impossible.
God says: All things are possible.
LUKE 18:27

You say: I'm too tired.
God says: I will give you rest.
MATTHEW 11:28–30

You say: Nobody really loves me.
God says: I love you.
JOHN 3:15

You say: I can't go on.
God says: My grace is sufficient.
2 CORINTHIANS 12:9

You say: I can't figure things out.
God says: I will direct your steps.
PROVERBS 3:5–6

You say: I can't do it.
God says: You can do all things.
PHILIPPIANS 4:13

You say: I'm not able.
God says: I am able.
2 CORINTHIANS 9:8

You say: It's not worth it.
God says: It will be worth it.
ROMANS 8:28

You say: I can't forgive myself.
God says: I forgive you.
1 JOHN 1:9

You say: I can't manage.
God says: I will supply all your needs.
PHILIPPIANS 4:19

You say: I'm afraid.
God says: I have not given you a spirit of fear.
2 TIMOTHY 1:7

You say: I'm always worried and frustrated.
God says: Cast all your cares on Me.
1 PETER 5:7

You say: I don't have enough faith.
God says: I've given everyone a measure of faith.
ROMANS 12:3

You say: I'm not smart enough.
God says: I give you wisdom.
1 CORINTHIANS 1:30

You say: I feel all alone.
God says: I will never leave you or forsake you.
HEBREWS 13:5

AUTHOR UNKNOWN

GOD IS...

Never late

Never unfaithful

Never cruel

Never absent

Never unloving

Never wrong

PAUL J. MEYER
FROM "UNLOCKING YOUR LEGACY"

OUR GOD CANNOT

† We may grow weary…
    but our God cannot,

† We may give up…
    but our God cannot,

† We may fluctuate…
    but our God cannot,

† We may vacillate…
    but our God cannot,

† We may disappoint ourselves…
    but our God cannot disappoint anyone,

† We may fail a thousand times…
    but our God cannot fail,
    not even once.

RAY PRITCHARD
FROM "THE GOD YOU CAN TRUST"

WHY?

I can...

Rest from the burden of a small god. *Why?*
Because I have found the Lord.

Rest from doing things my way. *Why?*
Because the Lord is my Shepherd.

Rest from endless wants. *Why?*
Because I shall not want.

Rest from weariness. *Why?*
Because He makes me to lie down.

Rest from worry. *Why?*
Because He leads me.

Rest from hopelessness. *Why?*
Because He restores my soul.

Rest from guilt. *Why?*
Because He leads me in the paths of righteousness.

Rest from arrogance. *Why?*
Because of His name's sake.

Rest from the valley of death. *Why?*
Because He walks me through it.

Rest from the shadow of grief. *Why?*
> **Because He guides me.**

Rest from fear. *Why?*
> **Because His presence comforts me.**

Rest from loneliness. *Why?*
> **Because He is with me.**

Rest from shame. *Why?*
> **Because He has prepared a place for me in the presence of my enemies.**

Rest from my disappointments. *Why?*
> **Because He anoints me.**

Rest from envy. *Why?*
> **Because my cup overflows.**

Rest from doubt. *Why?*
> **Because He follows me.**

Rest from homesickness. *Why?*
> **Because I will dwell in the house of my Lord forever.**

MAX LUCADO
FROM "TRAVELING LIGHT"

COMFORT AND JOY

◆ It's impossible to be always happy, but it really is possible to be continually joyful.

◆ Little joys can carry you through when you can't get your mind or body around big ones.

◆ You can *be* joyful even when you don't *feel* joyful. You can *accept* comfort even when you don't *feel* comfortable.

◆ When you don't feel comfort, look for strength. When you don't feel strong, give the Lord your weakness.

◆ Joy comes from understanding what has been promised, trusting in God's care, practicing thanksgiving—and appreciating life.

◆ God will give you the comfort and joy you need, in the proper dosages, to bring you where you need to be.

◆ Joy is that deep-down knowledge that all is well, regardless, and all shall be well, no matter what.

EMILIE BARNES
FROM "A DIFFERENT KIND OF MIRACLE"

IT IS POSSIBLE

→ *It is possible* to cast all our care upon Him daily and to enjoy deep peace in doing it.

→ *It is possible* to have the thoughts and imaginations of our hearts purified, in the deepest meaning of the word.

→ *It is possible* to see the will of God in everything, and to receive it, not with sighing, but with singing.

→ *It is possible* by taking complete refuge in divine power to become strong through and through.

H. C. G. MOULE
FROM "STREAMS IN THE DESERT"

WHEN I GROW OLD

Thoughts from Psalm 71

I will remember with wonder and thanks the thousands of
times I have leaned on God since my youth.
For you are my hope; O Lord GOD,
you are my confidence from my youth.

❧

I will take refuge in God rather than
taking offense at my troubles.
In You, O LORD, I have taken refuge.

❧

I will speak to God more and more (not less and less)
of all His greatness until there is no room
in my mouth for murmuring.
My praise is continually of You.

❧

I will hope (doggedly) and not give in to despair,
even in the nursing home,
and even if I outlive all my friends.
I will hope continually.

❧

I will find people to tell about God's wonderful
acts of salvation and never run out,
because they are innumerable.
My mouth shall tell of Your righteousness, and of Your
salvation all day long, for I do not know the sum of them.

I will stay on the lookout for younger people and tell them about the power of God. I will tell them that God is strong and can be trusted in youth and age.

Do not forsake me, until I declare
Your strength to this generation.

❧

I will remember that there are great things about God above my imagination, and soon enough I will know these too.

Your righteousness, O God, reaches to the heavens.

❧

I will count all my pain and trouble as a gift from God and a path to glory.

You who have shown me many troubles and distresses
will revive me again.

❧

I will resist stereotypes of old people, and play and sing and shout with joy (whether it looks dignified or not).

I will praise You with the harp, even Your truth,
O my God; to you I will sing praises with the lyre,
O Holy One of Israel.

JOHN PIPER
FROM "A GODWARD LIFE"
SCRIPTURE VERSES ARE FROM NEW AMERICAN STANDARD BIBLE

WHY WE LONG FOR HEAVEN

There are better things ahead than any we leave behind.
C. S. LEWIS

I shall hear in heaven.
LUDWIG VAN BEETHOVEN

Remember that when you leave this earth, you can take with you nothing that you have received—only what you have given.
ST. FRANCIS OF ASSISI

The heart longs for heaven, heaven longs for the heart.
KIMBER ANNE ENGSTROM

Today I am one day nearer home than ever before.
One day nearer the dawning when the fog will lift,
mysteries clear, and all question marks straighten up into
exclamation points!
VANCE HAVNER

*Though we live on earth we have already
established legal residence in heaven.*

ERWIN W. LUTZER

Our home in heaven is paved with welcome mats.

JULIA PENN

*We talk about heaven being so far away.
It is within speaking distance to those who belong there.*

DWIGHT L. MOODY

*The call of heaven is the sweetest music we will ever hear.
Its melody bids us to "come home."*

JUDY GORDON

Death is God's delightful way of giving us life.

OSWALD CHAMBERS

AT THE MOMENT OF DEATH

At the moment of death, spirits will be made perfect.
There will be no more sin in us. We will be done with the inner war
and the heartrending disappointments of offending the Lord who loved
us and gave Himself for us.

At the moment of death, we will be relieved of the pain of this world.
The joy of the resurrection [of our bodies] will not yet be ours, but the
joy of freedom from pain will be.

At the moment of death, we will be given profound rest in our souls.
There will be a serenity beneath the eye and care of God that surpasses
anything we have known here on the softest summer evening beside the
most peaceful lake at our most happy moments.

At the moment of death, we will experience a deep at-homeness.
The whole human race is homesick for God without knowing it. When
we go home to Christ there will be a contentment beyond any sense of
security and peace we have ever known.

At the moment of death, we will be with Christ.
Christ is a more wonderful person than anyone on earth. He is wiser,
stronger, and kinder than anyone you enjoy spending time with. He is
endlessly interesting. He knows exactly what to do and what to say at
every moment to make His guests as glad as they can possibly be.

He overflows with love…

JOHN PIPER
CONDENSED FROM "A GODWARD LIFE"

HEAVEN IS...

---

† Full of JOY

† Full of LIFE

† Full of PEACE

† Full of BEAUTY

† Full of LIGHT

† Full of GLORY

† Full of GOODNESS

† Full of LOVE

† Full of GOD

† Full of WONDER

† Full of WORSHIP

† Full of NEWNESS

ST. JOHN
FROM THE BOOK OF REVELATION

WHEN YOU THINK OF HEAVEN...

Think of—

Stepping on shore, and finding it heaven!

Taking hold of a hand, and finding it God's hand.

Breathing a new air, and finding it celestial air.

Feeling invigorated, and finding it immortality.

Passing from storm to tempest to an unbroken calm.

Waking up, and finding it home.

AUTHOR UNKNOWN

ALICE GRAY is an inspirational conference speaker and the compiler of the bestselling Stories for the Heart book series, with more than 7 million copies sold. She and her husband, Al, reside in Arizona.

STEVE STEPHENS is a licensed psychologist, marriage and family therapist, radio host, seminar speaker, and the author of seventeen books. Steve lives with his wife, Tami, and three children in Oregon.

JOHN VAN DIEST has been a book publisher for more than twenty-five years and is a recipient of the prestigious Publisher of the Year Award. He travels the world as an advocate for Christian literature. John lives with his wife, Pat, in Oregon.

Are you a Walk Out Woman?

There is an epidemic of women walking out on their marriages. In *The Walk Out Woman,* Dr. Steve Stephens and Alice Gray bring the expertise you need to uncover marital stressors and provide practical solutions to heal your relationship.

Are you a walk out woman? Find out! It could save your marriage.

"For any man who wants to love his wife more deeply— and for any woman who is dying to be loved that way."
—Neil Clark Warren, psychologist and founder, eHarmony.com

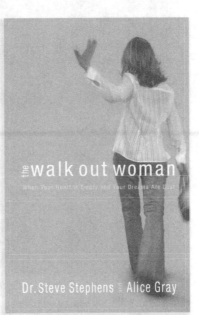

1-59052-267-2

To find out more, visit
www.multnomahbooks.com or www.thewornoutwoman.com

Life-Changing Advice in a
Quick-to-Read Format!

With sales of over 700,000 copies, the Lists to Live By series has something for everyone—guidance, inspiration, humor, family, love, health, and home. These books are perfect gifts for all occasions.

visit www.multnomahbooks.com | www.alicegray.com

LISTS TO LIVE BY FOR EVERY MARRIED COUPLE

Offers tender, romantic, and wise ways to bring new life to marriage in a popular, easy-to-read format! This special collection of Lists to Live By is filled with gems of inspiration and timeless truths that married couples will treasure for a lifetime.

ISBN 1-57673-998-8

LISTS TO LIVE BY FOR EVERY CARING FAMILY

Provides inspiration on how to love, teach, understand, uplift, and communicate with children on topics such as "Helping Your Child Succeed," "Pray for Your Children," and "Four Ways to Encourage Your Kids." Parents will cherish each nugget of truth in this timeless special collection of Lists to Live By.

ISBN 1-57673-999-6

LISTS TO LIVE BY FOR SIMPLE LIVING

In our fast-paced, complex world, we're all looking for stillness, harmony, gentleness, and peace. The beauty of these eighty thoughtfully chosen lists is that they use simplicity to bring you simplicity—condensing essential information into one or two page lists.

ISBN 1-59052-058-0

LISTS TO LIVE BY FOR SMART LIVING

Reading a list is like having the best parts of a whole book gathered into a few words. Each list is a simple path to a better—smarter—life! If you read them, use them, and live them, you will become successful where it really matters—family, friendship, health, finance, business, wisdom, and faith.

ISBN 1-59052-057-2

The Stories for the Heart Series

compiled by Alice Gray

Stories for the Extreme Teen's Heart ---------------------- ISBN 1-57673-703-9
Stories for a Teen's Heart, Book 1 -------------------------- ISBN 1-57673-646-6
Stories for a Teen's Heart, Book 2 -------------------------- ISBN 1-57673-797-7
Stories for a Teen's Heart, Book 3 -------------------------- ISBN 1-57673-974-0
Stories for a Faithful Heart -------------------------------- ISBN 1-57673-491-9
Stories for a Woman's Heart: The First Collection ------ ISBN 1-57673-474-9
Stories for a Woman's Heart: The Second Collection --- ISBN 1-57673-859-0
Stories for the Family's Heart ----------------------------- ISBN 1-57673-356-4
Stories for a Man's Heart ---------------------------------- ISBN 1-57673-479-X
Stories for the Heart: The Original Collection ---------- ISBN 1-57673-127-8
Stories for the Heart: The Second Collection ------------ ISBN 1-57673-823-X
Stories for the Heart: The Third Collection ------------- ISBN 1-57673-773-X

ACKNOWLEDGMENTS

Hundreds of books and magazines were researched and dozens of professionals interviewed for this collection. A diligent effort has been made to attribute original ownership of each list and, when necessary, obtain permission to reprint. If we have overlooked giving proper credit to anyone, please accept our apologies. If you will contact Multnomah Publishers, Inc., Post Office Box 1720, Sisters, Oregon 97759, with written documentation, corrections will be made prior to additional printings.

Notes and acknowledgments are shown in the order the lists appear in each section of the book. For permission to reprint a list, please request permission from the original source shown in the following bibliography. The editors gratefully acknowledge authors, publishers, and agents who granted permission for reprinting these lists.

FAITH

"The Ultimate Good in the 'Good News'" by John Piper adapted from *The Passion of Jesus Christ* by John Piper, copyright © 2004. Used by permission of Crossway Books, a division of Good News Publishers, Wheaton, IL 60187, www.crosswaybooks.org.

"If Jesus Is Your Savior" from *Just Give Me Jesus* by Anne Graham Lotz. Copyright © 2000, W. Publishing, Nashville, Tennessee. All rights reserved. Reprinted by permission.

"A Violent Grace" from *A Violent Grace* by Michael Card. Published by Multnomah Publishers, Inc., Sisters, Oregon. Copyright © 2001. Used by permission.

"Grace Means..." condensed from *In the Grip of Grace* by Max Lucado. Copyright © 1999, W. Publishing, Nashville, Tennessee. All rights reserved. Reprinted by permission.

"Intimacy with God" from *Simply Jesus* by Joseph M. Stowell. Published by Multnomah Publishers, Inc., Sisters, Oregon. Copyright © 2002. Used by permission.

"How to Listen to God" condensed from *How to Listen to God* by Charles Stanley. Copyright © 1985, W. Publishing, Nashville, Tennessee. All rights reserved. Reprinted by permission.

"Our Response to God" adapted from *What the Spirit Is Saying* by Henry Blackaby. Published by Multnomah Publishers, Inc., Sisters, Oregon. Copyright © 2003. Used by permission.

"God Is Worthy of Our Faith" by Lisa Tawn Bergren. Reprinted from *God Encounter*. Copyright © 2002 by Lisa Tawn Bergren. Used by permission of WaterBrook Press, Colorado Springs, CO. All rights reserved.

"Questions for Those Who Doubt" from *A Psalm in My Heart* by Leroy Brownlow. Copyright © 1989. Used by permission of Brownlow Publishing Company. All rights reserved.

"I See God in…" by Paul Ellison, pastor and Bible teacher. Copyright © 2004. Used by permission.

"Faith Is…" condensed from *Faith Is* by Pamela Reeve. Published by Multnomah Publishers, Inc., Sisters, Oregon. Copyright © 1999. Used by permission.

"What We Need" by Larry Libby and Steve Halliday. Reprinted from *No Matter What, No Matter Where*. Copyright © 2000 by Larry Libby and Steve Halliday. Used by permission of WaterBrook Press, Colorado Springs, CO. All rights reserved.

"50 Faith-Building Books" compiled by Alice Gray, Dr. Steve Stephens, and John Van Diest. Copyright © 2004. Used by permission.

GROWING DEEPER AND STRONGER

"God Will Reward You" condensed from *A Life God Rewards* by Bruce Wilkinson. Published by Multnomah Publishers, Inc., Sisters, Oregon. Copyright © 2002. Used by permission.

"Developing Self-Discipline" by John F. MacArthur condensed from *The Pillars of Christian Character* by John F. MacArthur, copyright © 1998. Used by permission of Crossway Books, a division of Good News Publishers, Wheaton, IL 60187, www.crosswaybooks.org.

"God Is Seeking You" from *The Air I Breathe* by Louis Giglio. Published by Multnomah Publishers, Inc., Sisters, Oregon. Copyright © 2003. Used by permission.

"Yielding to God" adapted from *Certain Peace in Uncertain Times* by Shirley Dobson. Published by Multnomah Publishers, Inc., Sisters, Oregon. Copyright © 2002. Used by permission.

"Spiritual Disciplines" by Dr. Steve Stephens, author and seminar speaker. Copyright © 2004. Used by permission.

"Six Steps to Spiritual Revival" from *Six Steps to Spiritual Revival* by Pat Robertson. Published by Multnomah Publishers, Inc., Sisters, Oregon. Copyright © 2002. Used by permission.

"The Value of Remembering" from *A Godward Life* by John Piper. Published by Multnomah Publishers, Inc., Sisters, Oregon. Copyright © 1997. Used by permission.

"10 Strategies to Strengthen Your Beliefs" from *Success God's Way* by Charles Stanley. Copyright © 2000, W. Publishing, Nashville, Tennessee. All rights reserved. Reprinted by permission.

"20 Tough Questions" from *Tough Questions* by Josh Warren. Copyright © 2002. Published by Group Publishing, Inc., Loveland, Colorado. www.grouppublishing.com. Used by permission.

"Desire for Spiritual Growth" adapted from *The Valley of Vision* by Arthur Bennett. Copyright © 1975. Published by Banner of Truth. Used by permission

"Guidelines for Giving" from *Standing on the Promises* by Susan Huey Wales. Published by Multnomah Publishers, Inc., Sisters, Oregon. Copyright © 2001. Used by permission.

"10 Principles of Discipline" adapted from *God Is In the Small Stuff* by Bruce Bickel and Stan Jantz. Copyright © 1998. Published by Promise Press. Used by permission.

GOD AND HIS WORD

"Who the Bible Says You Are" from *He Still Moves Stones* by Max Lucado. Copyright © 1993, W. Publishing, Nashville, Tennessee. All rights reserved. Reprinted by permission.

"What the Bible Does" by Loren Fischer, pastor and seminary professor. Copyright © 2004. Used by permission.

"Put the Bible in Your Heart" by Charles R. Swindoll, from the August 2000 issue of INSIGHTS Newsletter, © 2000. Published by Insight for Living, Plano, TX 75025. All rights reserved. Used by permission.

"Seven Steps for Memorizing Scripture" by Dr. Chad Garrison, pastor, Calvary Baptist Church, Lake Havasu City, Arizona. Copyright © 2004. Used by permission.

"A Gospel-Centered Life" condensed from *The Cross-Centered Life* by C. J. Mahaney. Published by Multnomah Publishers, Inc., Sisters, Oregon. Copyright © 2002. Used by permission.

"Applying Scripture to Your Life" by John Van Diest, associate publisher. Copyright © 2004. Used by permission.

"The Claims of Jesus" by Tim LaHaye from *Why Believe In Jesus?* Copyright © 2004 by Tim LaHaye. Published by Harvest House Publishers, Eugene, OR. Used by permission.

"The ABC's of God's Character" adapted from *When Children Pray* by Cheri Fuller. Published by Multnomah Publishers, Inc., Sisters, Oregon. Copyright © 1998. Used by permission.

"The Holy Spirit" condensed from *The Holy Spirit* by Max Lucado. Copyright © 1998, W. Publishing, Nashville, Tennessee. All rights reserved. Reprinted by permission.

"Truths About God" by Loren Fischer, pastor and seminary professor. Copyright © 2004. Used by permission.

"How God Responds" by Dr. Steve Stephens, author and seminar speaker. Copyright © 2004. Used by permission.

WORSHIP AND PRAISE

"Just Give Me Jesus" from *Just Give Me Jesus* by Anne Graham Lotz. Copyright © 2000, W. Publishing, Nashville, Tennessee. All rights reserved. Reprinted by permission.

"Seven Reasons Christ Suffered and Died" by John Piper adapted from *The Passion of Jesus Christ* by John Piper, copyright © 2004. Used by permission of Crossway Books, a division of Good News Publishers, Wheaton, IL 60187, www.crosswaybooks.org.

"Names of Jesus" condensed from *100 Portraits of Christ* by Henry Gariepy. Copyright © 1987. Used by permission of the author.

"God in Seven Tributes" from *A Psalm in My Heart* by Leroy Brownlow. Copyright © 1989. Used by permission of Brownlow Publishing Company. All rights reserved.

"Responding to God's Glory" by John Van Diest, associate publisher. Copyright © 2004. Used by permission.

"Honoring God's Holiness" by Dean Ridings adapted from *Focus on the Family* magazine, September 2001. Used by permission of the author. Dean Ridings is deputy director of communications for The Navigators and the author of numerous articles, devotionals, monographs, and plays. Dean lives in Colorado Springs, Colorado, with his wife and their four children.

"The Importance of Praise" adapted from *31 Days of Praise* by Ruth Meyers. Published by Multnomah Publishers, Inc., Sisters, Oregon. Copyright © 1994. Used by permission.

"Praise Changes Us" by Michael Youssef. Adapted from *Empowered by Praise*. Copyright © 2002 by Michael Youssef. Used by permission of WaterBrook Press, Colorado Springs, CO. All rights reserved.

"Daily Worship" condensed from *A Psalm in My Heart* by Leroy Brownlow. Copyright © 1989. Used by permission of Brownlow Publishing Company. All rights reserved.

"A Heart of Thanksgiving" from *Making Today Count for Eternity* by Kent Crockett. Published by Multnomah Publishers, Inc., Sisters, Oregon. Copyright © 2001. Used by permission.

"How to Press C-L-O-S-E-R to God" by Alice Gray, condensed from *The Worn Out Woman* by Dr. Steve Stephens and Alice Gray. Published by Multnomah Publishers, Inc., Sisters, Oregon. Copyright © 2004. Used by permission.

"The Purpose of Worship" by Geoffrey V. Guns, senior pastor, Second Calvary Baptist Church, Norfolk, Virginia, selected from his sermon, "The Purpose of Worship, Psalm 95:1–7." Copyright © 1996. Used by permission.

PRAYER

"He Is Able" by C. Samuel Storms from *Grandeur of God*. Copyright © 1984. Published by Baker Book House Company. Used by permission.

"Why Pray?" adapted from *Two Hearts Praying as One* by Dennis and Barbara Rainey. Published by Multnomah Publishers, Inc., Sisters, Oregon. Copyright © 2002. Used by permission.

"How to Pray" adapted from *Overcoming Overload* by Steve and Mary Farrar. Published by Multnomah Publishers, Inc., Sisters, Oregon. Copyright © 2003. Used by permission.

"Questions to Ask Before Praying" from *Too Busy Not to Pray* by Bill Hybels. Published by InterVarsity Press. Copyright © 1988, 1998. Used by permission.

"Four Ways God Answers Prayer" from *Too Busy Not to Pray* by Bill Hybels. Published by InterVarsity Press. Copyright © 1988, 1998. Used by permission.

"Six Reasons for Unanswered Prayer" from *Too Busy Not to Pray* by Bill Hybels. Published by InterVarsity Press. Copyright © 1988, 1998. Used by permission.

"What Happens When We Pray" from *Overcoming Overload* by Steve and Mary Farrar. Published by Multnomah Publishers, Inc., Sisters, Oregon. Copyright © 2003. Used by permission.

"Ways to Pray" from *When God Doesn't Heal Now* by Dr. Larry Keefauver. Copyright © 2002, W. Publishing, Nashville, Tennessee. All rights reserved. Reprinted by permission.

"What Prayer Provides" by John Van Diest, associate publisher. Copyright © 2004. Used by permission.

"The ABC's of Prayer" by Dusty, Dylan and Brittany Stephens. Copyright © 2004. Used by permission.

"Crying Out to God" condensed from *The Power of Crying Out* by Bill Gothard. Published by Multnomah Publishers, Inc., Sisters, Oregon. Copyright © 2002. Used by permission.

"Pray for Your Children" by Donna Otto taken from *Finding a Mentor, Being a Mentor.* Copyright © 2001 by Donna Otto. Published by Harvest House Publishers, Eugene, OR. Used by permission.

MARRIAGE

"Building a Marriage of Faith" by Charles R. Swindoll, from the August 2000 issue of INSIGHTS Newsletter, © 2000. Published by Insight for Living, Plano, TX 75025. All rights reserved. Used by permission.

"Praying for Your Wife" by Stormie Omartian taken from *The Power of a Praying Husband.* Copyright © 2001 by Stormie Omartian. Published by Harvest House Publishers, Eugene, OR. Used by permission.

"Praying for Your Husband" by Stormie Omartian taken from *The Power of a Praying Wife.* Copyright © 1997 by Stormie Omartian. Published by Harvest House Publishers, Eugene, OR. Used by permission.

"How to Love Your Wife" by Stuart Scott adapted from *The Exemplary Husband.* Copyright © 2002. Used by permission of Focus Publishing, Inc. All rights reserved.

"How to Love Your Husband" by Martha Peace condensed from *The Excellent Wife*. Copyright © 1999. Used by permission of Focus Publishing, Inc. All rights reserved.

"I Promise That…" by Fred Lowery condensed from *Covenant Marriage*. Copyright © 2002. Used by permission of Howard Publishing Company. All rights reserved.

"No Matter What Happens" by Gary and Barbara Rosberg from *Serving Love*. Copyright © 2003. Used by permission of Tyndale House Publishers. All rights reserved.

"Ten Things Every Wife Needs to Know" by Dan McAuley, college professor and marriage mentor. Copyright © 2004. Used by permission.

"Eight Things Every Husband Needs to Know" by Lysa TerKeurst from *Capture Her Heart*. Copyright © 2002. Used by permission of Moody Press. All rights reserved.

"The Proverbs 31 Marriage…for Wives" by Renee S. Sanford. Copyright © 2004. Used by permission. Renee Sanford is a wife, mother, friend, Bible teacher and speaker, book editor, feature writer, coauthor of the *Living Faith Bible* (Tyndale), and vice president of Sanford Communications, Inc., Portland, OR 97213, 503-239-5229, reneesanford@earthlink.net.

"The Proverbs 31 Marriage…for Husbands" by David Sanford. Copyright © 2004. Used by permission. David Sanford is a husband, father, friend, educator, editor, author, literary agent, coauthor of the *Living Faith Bible* (Tyndale) and *God Is Relevant* (Doubleday), and president of Sanford Communications, Inc., Portland, OR 97213, 503-239-5229, drsanford@earthlink.net.

"How Praying Together Can Help Your Marriage" from *Two Hearts Praying as One* by Dennis and Barbara Rainey. Published by Multnomah Publishers, Inc., Sisters, Oregon. Copyright © 2002. Used by permission.

"Six Steps for Handling Conflict" from *Night Light* by Dr. James and Shirley Dobson. Published by Multnomah Publishers, Inc., Sisters, Oregon. Copyright © 2000. Used by permission.

"When Your Loved One Doesn't Love God" by Nancy Kennedy condensed from *Marriage Partnership* magazine, Vol. 16. No. 1. Copyright © 1999. Used by permission of the author. Nancy Kennedy is the author of *When He Doesn't Believe* and *Between Two Loves*.

FAMILY

"10 Purposes of Parenting" by David Seel Jr. from *Parenting Without Perfection*. Copyright © 2000. Used by permission of NavPress, Colorado Springs, Colorado. All rights reserved.

"20 Ways to Bless Your Children" by Tim Kimmel condensed from *Legacy of Love*. Copyright © 1989. Used by permission of the author. Dr. Tim Kimmel is executive director of Family Matters. He has authored several books including

Grace-Based Parenting and *Little House on the Freeway*. You can learn more about Family Matters by visiting familymatters.net.

"Building Your Child's Faith" by Mary Maslen adapted from *Christian Parenting Today* magazine (Spring 2003), published by Christianity Today International, Carol Stream, Illinois. Used by permission of the author, Mary Maslen, early childhood development specialist. Most recent studies Harvard Graduate School of Education, Cambridge, MA.

"How to Raise Totally Awesome Kids" condensed from *How to Raise Totally Awesome Kids* by Dr. Chuck and Jenni Borsellino. Published by Multnomah Publishers, Inc., Sisters, Oregon. Copyright © 2002. Used by permission.

"When Parents Get Discouraged" from *Parenting Isn't for Cowards* by Dr. James Dobson. Published by Multnomah Publishers, Inc., Sisters, Oregon. Copyright © 1987. Used by permission.

"A Parent's Commitment to Prodigal Children" by Ruth Bell Graham from *Prodigals and Those Who Love Them*. Copyright © 1991, 1999. Published by Baker Book House Company. Used by permission.

"Eight Steps to Great Communication" by Dr. Kevin Leman adapted from *Making Children Mind Without Losing Yours*. Copyright © 2000. Published by Fleming H. Revell, a division of Baker Book House Company. Used by permission.

"Nurturing Compassion" by Tami Stephens, mother of three. Copyright © 2004. Used by permission.

"Give Children Love" by Donna Otto taken from *Finding a Mentor, Being a Mentor*. Copyright © 2001 by Donna Otto. Published by Harvest House Publishers, Eugene, OR. Used by permission.

"Connecting With Your Kids" by Kathi Hunter adapted from *Christian Parenting Today* magazine (Fall 2003), published by Christianity Today International, Carol Stream, Illinois. Used by permission of the author. Kathi Hunter is a popular Christian speaker and writer whose work has appeared in *Focus on the Family* magazine, *Today's Christian Woman*, and *Christian Parenting Today*. She is the adoring mom of two, Justen and Kimberly.

"Avoiding the Spending Trap" by Lisa Jackson adapted from *Christian Parenting Today* magazine (March/April 2002), published by Christianity Today International, Carol Stream, Illinois. Used by permission of the author.

"How to Stop Family Bickering" by Theresa B. Lode. This article first appeared in *Christian Parenting Today* magazine (Spring 2003), published by Christianity Today International, Carol Stream, Illinois. Theresa Lode is a freelance writer living in Montana. She is presently working on a humorous book on parenting.

"10 Ways to Teach Your Children Integrity" by Tim Kimmel from *Legacy of Love*. Copyright © 1989. Used by permission of the author. Dr. Tim Kimmel is executive director of Family Matters. He has authored several books including *Grace-Based Parenting* and *Little House on the Freeway*. You can learn more about Family Matters by visiting familymatters.net.

"10 Ways to Teach Your Child Discipline" by Tim Kimmel from *Legacy of Love*. Copyright © 1989. Used by permission of the author. Dr. Tim Kimmel is executive director of Family Matters. He has authored several books including *Grace-Based Parenting* and *Little House on the Freeway*. You can learn more about Family Matters by visiting familymatters.net.

"Helping Your Kids Succeed" by James M. Kouzes and Barry Z. Posner adapted from *Encouraging the Heart: A Leader's Guide to Rewarding and Recognizing Others*. Copyright © 1999 James M. Kouzes and Barry Z. Posner. This material is used by permission of John Wiley & Sons, Inc.

"Family Rules" by Dr. Rick and Jerilyn Fowler from *Christian Parenting Today* magazine (Summer 2002), published by Christianity Today International, Carol Stream, Illinois. Used by permission of the authors.

"Benefits of Less Television" by Kirsetin Karamarkovich Morello adapted from *Christian Parenting Today* magazine (Fall 2002), published by Christianity Today International, Carol Stream, Illinois. Used by permission of the author.

"Advice to Parents" by Annette Smith adapted from *Help! My Little Girl's Growing Up* Copyright © 2001 by Annette Smith. Published by Harvest House Publishers, Eugene, OR. Used by permission.

COMMUNITY

"The Walk of Love" from *A Gift of Love* by Charles Stanley. Copyright © 2002, W. Publishing, Nashville, Tennessee. All rights reserved. Reprinted by permission.

"Love Is…" by Barbara Johnson taken from *Fresh Elastic for Stretched Out Moms*. Copyright © 2003 by Barbara Johnson. Published by Fleming H. Revell, a division of Baker Book House Company. Used by permission.

"Be an Encourager" from *God Is In the Small Stuff* by Bruce Bickel and Stan Jantz. Copyright © 1998. Published by Promise Press. Used by permission.

"Give and Take" by David and Claudia Arp, adapted from *Marriage Partnership* magazine, Spring 2003. Used by permission of the authors. David and Claudia Arp, founders of Marriage Alive, are speakers and authors of numerous books including the *101 Great Dates* series and *The Second Half of Marriage*. Website: www.marriagealive.com

"Sharing 101" from *And When You Pray* by Ray Pritchard. Copyright © 2002. Published by Broadman and Holman Publishers. Used by permission.

"Five Reasons We Need Friends" condensed from *The Worn Out Woman* by Dr. Steve Stephens and Alice Gray. Published by Multnomah Publishers, Inc., Sisters, Oregon. Copyright © 2004. Used by permission.

"Relationships Will Struggle If…" by Michael L. Brown condensed from *Revolution in the Church*. Copyright © 2002. Published by Chosen Books, a division of Baker Book House Company. Used by permission.

"You Cause Others to Stumble When…" by Dr. Steve Stephens, author and seminar speaker. Copyright © 2004. Used by permission.

"When Anger Hurts Others" by John Van Diest, associate publisher. Copyright © 2004. Used by permission.

"What Caring Friends Will Do" by Alice Gray, author and seminar speaker. Copyright © 2004. Used by permission.

"Eight Reasons to Go to Church" by James A. Scudder from *Your Secret to Spiritual Success* by John Piper, copyright © 2002. Used by permission of Crossway Books, a division of Good News Publishers, Wheaton, IL 60187, www.crosswaybooks.org.

"Tips for Finding a Good Church" from *The Victorious Life* by Tony Evans. Copyright © 1994, W. Publishing, Nashville, Tennessee. All rights reserved. Reprinted by permission.

"Lifestyle Evangelism" by Dr. David Jeremiah adapted from *Turning Points,* Dr. David Jeremiah's bimonthly *Devotional* magazine. Call Turning Point at 1-800-947-1993 for your complimentary copy of Turning Points. Used by permission of the author.

"Becoming 'Fishers of Men'" from *Unashamed* by Floyd McElveen. Published by Multnomah Publishers, Inc., Sisters, Oregon. Copyright © 2003. Used by permission.

"Sharing the Gospel" condensed from *Unashamed* by Floyd McElveen. Published by Multnomah Publishers, Inc., Sisters, Oregon. Copyright © 2003. Used by permission.

SUCCESS

"Breaking Out of the Rut" by Rick Warren. This article is reprinted from the Website www.Pastors.com Copyright © 2004. Used by permission. All rights reserved.

"Eight Benefits of a Positive Attitude" by Paul J. Meyer from *Unlocking Your Legacy.* Copyright © 2002. Used by permission of Moody Press. All rights reserved.

"Eight Important Goals" from *Success God's Way* by Charles Stanley. Copyright © 2000, W. Publishing, Nashville, Tennessee. All rights reserved. Reprinted by permission.

"Tests for Decision Making" by June Hunt condensed from HOPE FOR THE HEART, *Biblical Counseling Key:* Decision Making. Copyright © 2002. Used by permission.

"21 Principles for Spiritual Leaders" condensed from *Spiritual Leadership* by Henry and Richard Blackaby. Copyright © 2001. Published by Broadman and Holman Publishers. Used by permission.

"The Role of Spiritual Leaders" condensed from *Spiritual Leadership* by Henry and Richard Blackaby. Copyright © 2001. Published by Broadman and Holman Publishers. Used by permission.

"Core Truths" by Emilie Barnes from *A Different Kind of Miracle*. Copyright © 2002 by Harvest House Publishers, Eugene, Oregon. Used by permission.

"Seven Deadly Sins" by Tony Campolo, author and speaker, from *Seven Deadly Sins*. Copyright © 1987. Used by permission.

"12 Secrets to Happiness" by Dr. Steve Stephens, author and seminar speaker. Copyright © 2004. Used by permission.

"Always Remember This" adapted from *God Is In the Small Stuff* by Bruce Bickel and Stan Jantz. Copyright © 1998. Published by Promise Press. Used by permission.

VIRTUES

"Why Settle for…" by Stephen Arterburn from *Flashpoints*. Copyright © 2002. Used by permission of Tyndale House Publishers. All rights reserved.

"How to Safeguard Your Character" from *The Paradox of Power* by Pat Williams. Copyright © 2002 by Pat Williams. By permission of Warner Books, Inc.

"Five Qualities That Change Your Heart" by Jerome Daily from *Soul Space*. Copyright © 2003. Published by Integrity Publishers. Used by permission.

"How to Live a Holy Life" by Dr. Chad Garrison, pastor, Calvary Baptist Church, Lake Havasu City, AZ. Copyright © 2004. Used by permission.

"Pride vs. Teachability" by Steven Mosley from *Secrets of the Mustard Seed*. Copyright © 2002. Used by permission of NavPress, Colorado Springs, Colorado. All rights reserved.

"The Value of Integrity" from *Communicate* by Terry Brown and Michael Ross. Copyright © 2002. Published by Promise Press. Used by permission.

"Protecting Your Integrity" by Pat Williams from *How to Be Like Jesus*. Copyright © 2003. Used by permission of Health Communications, Inc.

"If You Bypass Virtue" by Dr. Steve Stephens, author and seminar speaker. Copyright © 2004. Used by permission.

"Avoid These Common Sins" by Luis Palau from *Say Yes! How to Renew Your Spiritual Passion*. Copyright © 2000. Used by permission. Luis Palau is a world-renowned evangelist, broadcaster, and author of 45 books. Luis Palau serves as president of the Luis Palau Evangelist Association, P.O. Box 1173, Portland, OR 97207, www.palau.org, lpea@palau.org.

"Scriptures That Communicate Virtue" by Scott Turansky and Joanne Miller. Reprinted from *Good and Angry*. Copyright © 2002 by Effective Parenting, Inc. Used by permission of WaterBrook Press, Colorado Springs, CO. All rights reserved.

"Power Principles for Christian Service" by David and Warren W. Wiersbe from *Making Sense of the Ministry*. Copyright © 1997, published by Baker Book House. Used by permission of the authors.

"What Faithfulness Means" condensed from *Making Today Count for Eternity* by Kent Crockett. Published by Multnomah Publishers, Inc., Sisters, Oregon. Copyright © 2001. Used by permission.

"Turning Foes into Friends" by June Hunt condensed from HOPE FOR THE HEART, *Biblical Counseling Key*: Anger. Copyright © 2002. Used by permission.

"What Forgiveness Does" from *Two Hearts Praying as One* by Dennis and Barbara Rainey. Published by Multnomah Publishers, Inc., Sisters, Oregon. Copyright © 2002. Used by permission.

"Seven Steps of Forgiveness" by Alice Gray from *The Walk Out Woman*. Copyright © 2004. Published by Multnomah Publishers, Inc., Sisters, Oregon. Used by permission.

"Random Acts of Righteousness" condensed from *Making Today Count for Eternity* by Kent Crockett. Published by Multnomah Publishers, Inc., Sisters, Oregon. Copyright © 2001. Used by permission.

COMFORT FOR THE TOUGH TIMES

"Four Things That Make Trials Easier" by Ruth Bell Graham from *Prodigals and Those Who Love Them*. Copyright © 1991, 1999. Published by Baker Book House Company. Used by permission.

"The Comforter" from *Just Give Me Jesus* by Anne Graham Lotz. Copyright © 2000, W. Publishing, Nashville, Tennessee. All rights reserved. Reprinted by permission.

"God Can!" by Geoffrey V. Guns, senior pastor, Second Calvary Baptist Church, Norfolk, Virginia, selected from his sermon, "The Purpose of Worship, Psalm 95:1–7." Copyright © 1996. Used by permission.

"The Good Shepherd" from *Till Armageddon* by Billy Graham. Copyright © 1981, W. Publishing, Nashville, Tennessee. All rights reserved. Reprinted by permission.

"Where to Look" by Glenda Hotton, professor of home economics, The Master's College. Copyright © 2004. Used by permission.

"When Going Through Difficulties…" by Ray Pritchard from *The God You Can Trust*. Copyright © 2003 by Ray Pritchard. Published by Harvest House Publishers, Eugene, OR. Used by permission.

"Healing Your Emotional Wounds" taken from *On-Purpose Leadership* by Dale Galloway. Copyright © 2001 by Beacon Hill Press of Kansas City. All rights reserved. Used by permission of the publisher.

"How to R-E-S-T from Worry" by Brenda L. Whealey from *The Best Thing I Ever Did for My Marriage* by Nancy Cob and Connie Grigsby. Copyright © 2003. Published by Multnomah Publishers, Inc., Sisters, Oregon. Copyright © 2001. Used by permission of the author.

"12 Ways to Overcome Discouragement" by Renee S. Sanford. Copyright © 2004. Used by permission. Renee Sanford is a wife, mother, friend, Bible teacher and speaker, book editor, feature writer, coauthor of the *Living Faith Bible* (Tyndale), and vice president of Sanford Communications, Inc., Portland, OR 97213, 503-239-5229, reneesanford@earthlink.net.

"Showing God's Love" from *He's Gonna Toot and I'm Gonna Scoot* by Barbara Johnson. Copyright © 1999, W. Publishing, Nashville, Tennessee. All rights reserved. Reprinted by permission.

"When Our Children Disappoint Us" by Barbara Baumgardner, author of *Passage Through Grief,* adapted from *Decision* magazine, Oct. 1998. Used by permission.

"Seven Lessons from Job" by Dr. F. LaGard Smith taken from *The Daily Bible,* commentary by F. LaGard Smith. Copyright © 1984 by Harvest House Publishers, Eugene, OR. Used by permission.

ETERNAL HOPE

"God Is There" by Dr. Steve Stephens, author and seminar speaker. Copyright © 2004. Used by permission.

"Six Events in Your Forever Life" from *A Life God Rewards* by Bruce Wilkinson. Published by Multnomah Publishers, Inc., Sisters, Oregon. Copyright © 2002. Used by permission.

"Eternal Eyesight" by June Hunt condensed from HOPE FOR THE HEART, *Biblical Counseling Key:* Aging. Copyright © 2002. Used by permission.

"How Hope Acts" by Father James Keller, M.M., used by permission of The Christophers, 12 East 48th Street, New York, NY 10017.

"God Is..." by Paul J. Meyer from *Unlocking Your Legacy.* Copyright © 2002. Used by permission of Moody Press. All rights reserved.

"Our God Cannot" by Ray Pritchard taken from *The God You Can Trust.* Copyright © 2003 by Ray Pritchard. Published by Harvest House Publishers, Eugene, OR. Used by permission.

"Why?" from *Traveling Light* by Max Lucado. Copyright © 2001, W. Publishing, Nashville, Tennessee. All rights reserved. Reprinted by permission.

"Comfort and Joy" by Emilie Barnes taken from *A Different Kind of Miracle.* Copyright © 2002 by Emilie Barnes. Published by Harvest House Publishers, Eugene, OR. Used by permission.

"When I Grow Old" from *A Godward Life* by John Piper. Published by Multnomah Publishers, Inc., Sisters, Oregon. Copyright © 1997. Used by permission.

"At the Moment of Death" from *A Godward Life* by John Piper. Published by Multnomah Publishers, Inc., Sisters, Oregon. Copyright © 1997. Used by permission.